Mobility & Politics

Series Editors
Martin Geiger
Carleton University
Ottawa, Canada

Nicola Piper
School of Law
Queen Mary University of London
London, UK

Parvati Raghuram
Open University
Milton Keynes, UK

Editorial Board
Tendayi Bloom
University of Birmingham
Birmingham, UK

Michael Collyer
University of Sussex
Brighton, UK

Charles Heller
Graduate Institute
Geneva, Switzerland

Elaine Ho
National University of Singapore
Singapore, Singapore

Shadia Husseini de Araújo
University of Brasília
Brasília, Brazil

Alison Mountz
Wilfrid Laurier University
Waterloo, Canada

Linda Oucho
African Migration and Development Policy Centre
Nairobi, Kenya

Marta Pachocka
SGH Warsaw School of Economics
Warsaw, Poland

Antoine Pécoud
Université Sorbonne Paris Nord
Villetaneuse, France

Shahamak Rezaei
University of Roskilde
Roskilde, Denmark

Sergey Ryazantsev
Russian Academy of Sciences
Moscow, Russia

Carlos Sandoval García
University of Costa Rica
San José, Costa Rica

Everita Silina
The New School
New York, NY, USA

Rachel Simon-Kumar
University of Auckland
Auckland, New Zealand

William Walters
Carleton University
Ottawa, Canada

MOBILITY & POLITICS

SERIES EDITORS:
MARTIN GEIGER, CARLETON UNIVERSITY, OTTAWA, CANADA
Nicola Piper, Queen Mary University of London, UK
Parvati Raghuram, Open University, Milton Keynes, UK

Global Advisory Board:
Tendayi Bloom, University of Birmingham, UK
Michael Collyer, Sussex University, UK
Charles Heller, Geneva Graduate Institute, Switzerland
Elaine Ho, National University of Singapore
Shadia Husseini de Araújo, University of Brasília, Brazil
Alison Mountz, Wilfrid Laurier University, Waterloo, Canada
Linda Oucho, African Migration and Development Policy Centre, Nairobi, Kenya
Marta Pachocka, SGH Warsaw School of Economics, Poland
Antoine Pécoud, Sorbonne University Paris Nord, France
Shahamak Rezaei, University of Roskilde, Denmark
Sergey Ryazantsev, Russian Academy of Sciences, Moscow, Russia
Carlos Sandoval García, University of Costa Rica
Everita Silina, The New School, New York, USA
Rachel Simon-Kumar, University of Auckland, New Zealand
William Walters, Carleton University, Ottawa, Canada

Human mobility, whatever its scale, is often controversial. Hence it carries with it the potential for politics. A core feature of mobility politics is the tension between the desire to maximise the social and economic benefits of migration and pressures to restrict movement. Transnational communities, global instability, advances in transportation and communication, and concepts of 'smart borders' and 'migration management' are just a few of the phenomena transforming the landscape of migration today. The tension between openness and restriction raises important questions about how different types of policy and politics come to life and influence mobility.

Mobility & Politics invites original, theoretically and empirically informed studies for academic and policy-oriented debates. Authors examine issues such as refugees and displacement, migration and citizenship, security and cross-border movements, (post-)colonialism and mobility, and transnational movements and cosmopolitics.

This series is indexed in Scopus.

Diego Caballero-Vélez

Contesting Migration Crises in Central Eastern Europe

A Political Economy Approach to Poland's Responses Towards Refugee Protection Provision

Diego Caballero-Vélez
Centre of Migration Research (University of Warsaw)
Warsaw, Poland

ISSN 2731-3867　　　　　　ISSN 2731-3875　(electronic)
Mobility & Politics
ISBN 978-3-031-44036-6　　　ISBN 978-3-031-44037-3　(eBook)
https://doi.org/10.1007/978-3-031-44037-3

© The Editor(s) (if applicable) and The Author(s), under exclusive licence to Springer Nature Switzerland AG 2023

This work is subject to copyright. All rights are solely and exclusively licensed by the Publisher, whether the whole or part of the material is concerned, specifically the rights of translation, reprinting, reuse of illustrations, recitation, broadcasting, reproduction on microfilms or in any other physical way, and transmission or information storage and retrieval, electronic adaptation, computer software, or by similar or dissimilar methodology now known or hereafter developed.

The use of general descriptive names, registered names, trademarks, service marks, etc. in this publication does not imply, even in the absence of a specific statement, that such names are exempt from the relevant protective laws and regulations and therefore free for general use.

The publisher, the authors, and the editors are safe to assume that the advice and information in this book are believed to be true and accurate at the date of publication. Neither the publisher nor the authors or the editors give a warranty, expressed or implied, with respect to the material contained herein or for any errors or omissions that may have been made. The publisher remains neutral with regard to jurisdictional claims in published maps and institutional affiliations.

This Palgrave Macmillan imprint is published by the registered company Springer Nature Switzerland AG.
The registered company address is: Gewerbestrasse 11, 6330 Cham, Switzerland

Paper in this product is recyclable.

En des temps comme ceux-ci, la fuite est le seul moyen pour se maintenir vifs et continuer à rêve.
—Henri Laborit

To those who flee from adversity and persevere through unimaginable circumstances, I dedicate this work to you. Your indomitable spirit in the face of immense suffering serves as a poignant reminder of the urgent need for comprehensive and compassionate solutions to address migration crises.

ACKNOWLEDGEMENTS

This monograph stands as a profound acknowledgement of the unwavering support and inspiration of the remarkable individuals who have been instrumental in shaping my path in European and migration studies. Their encouragement, guidance, and camaraderie have enriched my academic journey beyond measure. This work represents the culmination of my efforts to explore and understand the complexities of refugee protection during critical junctures. My pursuit in this field began during the 2015 refugee crisis, a pivotal moment when the European Union grappled with the challenge of irregular migration. It was during this time that I observed the EU's call for protection burden-sharing among its Member States. Among them, the Visegrad Group countries, including Poland, stood in opposition, expressing their reluctance towards the relocation scheme and adopting a securitised political narrative surrounding refugees. This polarising landscape ignited my curiosity and propelled me to investigate further. It was during this year that under the supervision and guidance of Florian Trauner, Ilke Adam, and Christof Roos, I ignited my passion for this field. Their insights laid the foundation for my exploration, spurring me to delve deeper into the complexities of migration policy dynamics. The opportunity to pursue my doctoral studies under the guidance of Enrico Calossi and Marta Pachocka was a turning point in my career. Marta, in particular, has been an invaluable milestone in my journey as a migration expert. Her mentorship and unwavering support nurtured my interest in the Central Eastern European region and propelled me to new heights of understanding. The stimulating atmosphere at the Institute of European Studies (Université Libre de Bruxelles), fostered by Ramona

Coman, Frederik Ponjaert, and Maria Isabel Soldevilla, provided the perfect platform for engaging in profound conversations about the challenges of academic research. Their encouragement and engagement shaped my perspective and fuelled my dedication to my research academic path. The colleagues at the Centre of Migration Research at the University of Warsaw are a constant source of inspiration. Their valuable feedback on migration crises situations and dynamics continually broadens my knowledge, and working alongside them is an enriching experience. Jim Roberts, a milestone in my journey of understanding public goods theory, expanded my horizons in applying this political economy framework to the intricate realm of migration. His expertise has been transformative in my research endeavours. I am grateful to Leiza Brumat whose encouragement emboldened me in the process of writing this book. Her invaluable feedback on numerous aspects of my research has been pivotal in shaping my work. To my former PhD colleagues and friends, your unwavering encouragement to find balance, even amidst approaching deadlines, has been a lifeline. Your camaraderie has made this journey more joyful and fulfilling. To Giulia, whose unwavering support was a comforting embrace when the challenges seemed insurmountable. Your belief in my potential and your genuine happiness for my achievements brightened even the toughest day. To my family, you have been the bedrock of my strength and the source of inspiration. Your belief in my abilities, even when I doubted myself, kept me pushing forward. Your understanding during late nights of research and writing and the joyous celebrations after every milestone have made this experience all the more meaningful. To my dear grandparents, your wisdom and love continue to guide me, the values you instilled in me have shaped the person I am today, and I carry your legacy in every step of my professional and personal life. Last but not least, to the Mobility and Politics Series editors for having considered this book for publication and the reviewers for their valuable feedback.

Special mention to Isa, thank you for everything.

Contents

1 **Introduction**   1
  Migration Crises in Europe and the Securitisation of EU
  Migration Policy   1
  The Need for a New Theoretical Framework   5
  References   9

2 **International Cooperation in Public Goods Provision**   11
  Introduction   11
  Goods Typology   12
    Publicness Typology   13
    Globalness Typology   15
  Game Theory and 'Burden-Sharing' in Public Goods Provision   18
  Conclusions   22
  References   23

3 **Constructing Public Goods: Actors' Rationales Behind Actions**   27
  Introduction   27
  Maximising Benefits: Rational Choice Reasoning   28
  A Heuristic Alternative: Constructivist Reasoning   31
    The Identity-Utility Model   33
  Collective Action Failure Paradox   36
  Conclusions   41
  References   42

xiii

4 'Unpacking' International Migration Governance:
   Embeddedness and Political Economy   45
   Introduction   45
   International Migration Governance   46
   International Asylum Regime   49
      Refugee Protection as a Global Public Good   49
      The Positivist Maximising Utility Model   51
      The Identity Utility-Model   53
   The EU Migration Regime   54
      The Regulation of Refugee Protection as a European Public
      Good   56
   Conclusions   59
   References   60

5 Security or Humanitarianism? The Paradigm of Refugee
   Protection on Central-Eastern European Borders   65
   Introduction   65
   The 2021 Poland-Belarus Border Crisis: A Security Response   67
   The 2022 Ukrainian Refugee Crisis: A Humanitarian Response   69
   Conclusions   71
   References   72

6 Poland: Nation-building, Populism, and Ethnicity   73
   Introduction   73
   The Polish Party System and its Evolution Since 1989   74
      Polish Ruling Political Parties (2004–2020): The Birth of the
      Two-Party System   76
   The Rise of National-Conservative Populism in Poland   77
      Poland's Identity: Law and Justice's 'Re-vision' of the Polish
      Nation   78
      The Identity of the 'Other': European Identity vs. Polish Identity 79
   Polish Nation-Building Projects and Migration Policies   83
   Conclusions   86
   References   87

7 Modelling Preferences towards Refugee Protection: The Polish Government Case 91
Introduction 91
Framing Migration 92
The Identity-Utility Model: Framing Security and Humanitarianism 94
The Identity Utility Model: The Polish Case 97
   Framing Benefits and Costs 98
   The Multicultural Frame: Prestige and Development Benefits 99
Conclusions 100
References 101

8 Empirical Results: The (Non-) Provision of Refugee Protection 103
Data and Content Analysis 103
Eastern European Migrants: A Multicultural Narrative 120
Middle Eastern Migrants: A Nationalistic Narrative 122

9 Conclusion: Security and Humanitarian Preferences in Refugee Protection 127

Appendix A: Codebook 133

Appendix B: Politicians' Speeches 135

Appendix C: Law and Justice party manifesto 141

Appendix D: Parliamentary debates 145

Appendix E: Interviews 149

Appendix F: Interviews' Scenario 155

Index 161

LIST OF DIAGRAMS

Diagram 3.1	Agent's action process. (Source: Own elaboration)	30
Diagram 3.2	Case 1. (Source: Own elaboration)	33
Diagram 3.3	Altercasting process. (Source: Own elaboration)	35
Diagram 3.4	The provision of international security as a public good. (Source: Own elaboration)	40
Diagram 4.1	A state's construction of preferences. (Source: Own elaboration)	53
Diagram 6.1	Law and Justice's dimension of action. (Source: Own elaboration)	85
Diagram 6.2	Law and Justice's dimension of action (migration case). (Source: Own elaboration)	86
Diagram 7.1	The inductive process. (Source: Own elaboration)	93

List of Figures

Fig. 4.1	Pyramid of the EU asylum regime. (Source: Own elaboration, based on Langford (2013))	57
Fig. 8.1	Matrix frequency of international prestige benefit (PS). (Source: Own elaboration)	108
Fig. 8.2	Matrix frequency of the security benefit (PS). (Source: Own elaboration)	109
Fig. 8.3	Matrix frequency of the development benefit (PS). (Source: Own elaboration)	109
Fig. 8.4	Matrix frequency of the international prestige benefit (MP). (Source: Own elaboration)	111
Fig. 8.5	Matrix frequency of the security benefit (PS). (Source: Own elaboration)	112
Fig. 8.6	Matrix frequency of the international prestige frame (PD). (Source: Own elaboration)	113
Fig. 8.7	Matrix frequency of the security benefit frame (PD). (Source: Own elaboration)	115
Fig. 8.8	Matrix frequency of the development benefit frame (PD). (Source: Own elaboration)	115
Fig. 8.9	Matrix frequency of the international prestige benefit frame (I). (Source: Own elaboration)	117
Fig. 8.10	Matrix frequency of the security benefit frame (I). (Source: Own elaboration)	118

Fig. 8.11　Matrix frequency of the development benefit frame (I). (Source: Own elaboration) 119
Fig. 8.12　Sub-frames for Eastern European migrants. (Source: Own elaboration) 122
Fig. 8.13　Sub-frames for Middle Eastern migrants. (Source: Own elaboration) 124

List of Tables

Table 3.1	Characteristics of rational choice and constructivism in public goods *provision*	38
Table 7.1	Habermas framing model	95
Table 7.2	Identity-utility model frames in migration	96
Table 7.3	Identity-utility model for Law and Justice	98
Table 7.4	The identity-utility model in refugee protection provision	99
Table 7.5	The multicultural and nationalistic frames regarding prestige and security	100
Table 7.6	The multicultural frame regarding development benefits	100
Table 7.7	The security public good frame	101
Table 8.1	Example of framing with NVivo software	105
Table 8.2	Matrix- frames frequency of use (PS)	106
Table 8.3	Matrix- frames frequency of use Party manifesto (PM)	110
Table 8.4	Matrix- frames frequency of use Parliamentary debates (PD)	113
Table 8.5	Matrix- frames frequency of use (I)	116
Table 8.6	Matrix-frames frequency of use (data)-public goods	121
Table 8.7	Matrix- frames frequency of use (data)–development	121
Table 8.8	Matrix-frames frequency of use (data)—public goods	123
Table 8.9	Matrix- frames frequency of use (data)–private good	124

CHAPTER 1

Introduction

MIGRATION CRISES IN EUROPE AND THE SECURITISATION OF EU MIGRATION POLICY

In 1997, the Schengen Convention was incorporated into the mainstream of EU law by the Amsterdam Treaty. It came into effect in 1999 with the abolition of internal border controls in the EU, a milestone in the European integration project. In the meantime, due to the Yugoslav wars, nearly 700,000 asylum applications were filed in European countries, provoking a major refugee crisis (Wanner, 2002). During this period, the opening of Eastern Europe fostered more cooperation and policymaking at the EU level in migration issues. This led to the adoption of 'temporary protection' policies and the development of the European Asylum System for humanitarian protection. Such cooperation offered regularisation, rights, and security to individuals fleeing a conflict (Selm-Thorburn, 1998). After the post-war period, Western Europe's asylum regime enjoyed a period of stability (Thielemann, 2003). In the early 1990s, the Yugoslav wars led to a major refugee crisis, giving way to some changes. During this time, countries across Europe moved to introduce far-reaching restrictions into their domestic asylum legislation (Lavenex, 2001). Despite this, most observers agreed that this freedom of movement in the internal space of the EU required harmonised policy for the EU's external borders, and for so-called third-country nationals who were legally

© The Author(s), under exclusive license to Springer Nature Switzerland AG 2023
D. Caballero-Vélez, *Contesting Migration Crises in Central Eastern Europe*, Mobility & Politics,
https://doi.org/10.1007/978-3-031-44037-3_1

1

resident, but not nationals of one of the Member States. For this policy harmonisation to become reality, in 1990 the Dublin Convention was ratified, coming into effect in 1997. It had as the main objective preventing the submission of applications for asylum in multiple Member States.

In 2003, the Dublin Convention was replaced by the Dublin Regulation, becoming one of the cornerstones of the European Union's (EU) internal security acquis (Thielemann & Amstrong, 2013). As far as migration has started to be an internal security concern for the Member States, the Dublin Regulation's aim has been to cover issues of border control, asylum, and irregular migration as these are closely linked to the Schengen free-movement provisions (Thielemann & Amstrong, 2013). Political integration at the EU level might be altered with the emergence of existential threats. Some areas of European cooperation can be transformed when a 'critical juncture' occurs, for instance, a migration crisis (Huysmans, 2000). When that occurs, Member States could see migration as a threat, modifying their national interests and altering their willingness to embrace international cooperation. In the field of international relations studies, scholars investigating changes in policy and institutions in Europe typically employ either a multi-level governance framework or the new institutionalism theory. Strong integration is therefore understood as the efforts to substitute national regimes with common EU policies and to commit the Member States to narrowly implementing the EU rules.

Migration tends to be viewed primarily through the lens of securitisation in studies since the 1980s. The threats apparently posed by migration to both national sovereignty and human security are largely reflected in much of the recent academic literature (Thompson, 2013). In particular, the authors write about irregular migration, which is increasingly perceived by the governments and citizens of wealthier countries as a security threat (Collier, 2014). One of the central issues in both political and academic debates on migration policy and security highlights that if migration is dealt with as a security threat, a certain reluctance at supranationalisation can be noticed, notwithstanding the value of completely harmonised policies among the Member States (Ceccorulli, 2009). On this subject, Zincone and Caponio (2006) show that the specific analysis of migration policymaking is an even younger field of research. In this, scientific investigations pose the question of how immigration and integration policies are created, operationalised, and implemented. This does not focus on the content or frames of these policies *per se*, but on the political process through which such policies come into existence and how their implementation is steered. So, there is scrutiny of migration policy-making at both the EU and the national levels to know the type of policies that are made and, consequently, to what extent these are linked to the 'perception of threat' of the actors involved. EU Member States' cooperation on issues of internal security, border security, asylum, and, in particular, irregular immigration have raised several questions regarding the nature of such cooperation (Thielemann & Amstrong, 2013). The 2015 Syrian refugee crisis led to securitisation of the EU asylum regime and scepticism by some Member States towards the EU as a problem-solving institution. What is the focus of analysis, however, is the emergence and stability of agreements, such as the Dublin Convention, in light of this securitisation of EU asylum and migration policy areas (Thielemann & Amstrong, 2013). The European asylum and migration decision-making process has enabled national governments to strengthen their own domestic position at the EU level in a strategic way and to initiate processes of vertical and horizontal policy transfer (Thielemann, 2003). So far, under a European integration perspective, one may argue that European integration has helped national governments to overcome established institutional constraints and facilitated asylum and migration policy changes at the national level (Thielemann, 2003). This raises the question of to what extent the new securitised European asylum developments and policy changes may be explained by a European integration approach, as some Member States are reluctant to empower EU institutions in the asylum policy area when it comes to seeing migration as a problem of internal security.

In 2015 and 2016, the EU faced one of the most significant challenges in its recent history: the refugee crisis. This situation led the EU to put an emphasis on foreign policy tools in implementing solutions to resolve the crisis. This was reflected in migration being moved to the priorities in the external action agenda. This externalisation process with a security nature in its policy implementation led to the primary goal becoming tackling migration at its root causes, followed by strengthening cooperation with third countries, fighting people smuggling in countries of origin and transit states, and civil operations to combat human trafficking, and other actions. This securitisation process provoked an 'externalisation' of the policy itself. The question remains whether this 'policy transfer' from the domestic arena to an external dimension retains the goal of deeper integration of the migration and asylum regime. While the Member States differ on migration matters, they express common interests regarding the Common Security and

Defence Policy (CSDP). The EU, in transferring migration as a security aspect to external action, is reflected in several important policy documents, including the 2016 Global Strategy for Foreign and Security Policy in which migration and displacement are considered security challenges. In 2020, the European Commission launched the New Pact on Migration (NPM), a strong attempt to reinforce the Common European Asylum System (CEAS). In terms of 'resettlement', the Pact expounds on the concept of 'flexible solidarity', a term that provides room for the Member States to support each other in case of a massive influx of refugees. Instead of the 'mandatory' 2015 quota system by which each Member State was to take in a specific number of relocated refugees, under the NPM, the Member States may offer relocation, financing, support for EU agencies, and other 'solidarity' actions. Looking at a recent joint statement from the Visegrad countries (the Czech Republic, Hungary, Poland, and Slovakia) regarding the NPM, it is interesting to see that while they still perceive migration through a security lens, they are using a more humanitarian narrative in referring to the 2015 relocation scheme. In addition, the NPM tables the 'external' nature of migration. Both the terms 'solidarity' and 'external dimension' used in the Pact may be perceived as Brussels aiming to overcome collective action problems to strengthen the migration and asylum regime. In looking at the recent developments in the political crisis, it seems that externalisation of the migration situation has made it an external action problem rather than an intra-EU dispute. During the 2021 Poland-Belarus humanitarian border crisis, there was a change of narrative from the Polish government in which Prime Minister Mateusz Morawiecki decried Belarus's attempts to destabilise Europe and called on the Member States to stand together to defend Europe. Politicians of the ruling Law and Justice (*Prawo i Sprawiedliwość*) party saw those political tensions as a threat to Poland's national territory and sought to use the crisis as a uniting feature in a mutual stand against threats from Belarus and Russia. This border crisis showed that migration is within the external competences of the EU. Subsequently, the Member States (included the V4 countries) have been showing an 'open door' policy towards Ukrainian refugees, fleeing Russian aggression. Until recently, EU migration and asylum policy suffered disintegration rather than integration, mostly inflicted by the Central-Eastern European Member States. In contrast, providing refugee protection to Ukrainians may be seem as the EU's attempts to show unity towards a common threat—Russia. If the influx of Ukrainian refugees is treated purely in the foreign and defence dimension, the Central-Eastern European Member States may reinforce their position towards Brussels in migration and asylum issues. However, notwithstanding these important recent developments and the presence of a framework for cooperation, European asylum governance remains structured at the national level. In European asylum policies, the Member States have displayed that their policies are driven by mainly national interests rather than collective ones (see Zaun, 2017). European initiatives have so far not produced the expected effects on cooperation to face up to irregular migration, and most of the responses have been at the national level or though ad-hoc cooperation. In other words, European asylum governance is characterised by inter-state cooperation and national actions (mostly from European frontline states).

THE NEED FOR A NEW THEORETICAL FRAMEWORK

The new institutionalism approach has been used by scholars to explain policy change. Within its framework, the argument has been that 'the relative stability of Europe's post-war asylum regime can be accounted for by the fact that policymakers in this area are faced with strong international (e.g. human rights norms) and domestic (courts, constitutions, among others) institutional constraints, explaining the far-reaching changes introduced in the early 1990s' (Thielemann, 2003). For rational-choice theorists, institutions constitute a strategic operating environment, and they tend to regard institutions primarily as constraints on rational actors. The logic of expected consequences is the most commonly accepted framework for the interpretation of political events. In recent decades, rational choice institutionalism has been in a privileged position as a way to tell us something about how institutions can have a constraining effect on actors, and especially how policies may change due to those constraints (Thielemann, 2003). In trying to account for policy changes in the early 1990s, it is important to go beyond the analysis of factors that concern changes in the external environment of European states (Selm-Thorburn, 1998) and to look at the evolving European cooperation on asylum and immigration as a further important causal factor for changes in the Member States' asylum policies, a factor that has so far received insufficient attention in the literature (Thielemann, 2003). The recent concerns surrounding refugee migration flows, particularly as they relate to internal security, raise questions about the adequacy of relying solely on new institutionalism and European integration perspectives to understand changes in asylum and migration policies. The mainstream theoretical approaches, rooted in new institutionalism and European integration theories, have often been employed by scholars to analyze policy changes at both national and supranational levels over the past decades. However, these approaches may fall short in explaining why certain Member States do not enhance cooperation in EU-level asylum and migration policy areas. The slowdown of the European integration project, triggered by various crises in different EU policy domains following the 2008 financial crisis, has added complexity to the process of competences shifting from Member States to EU institutions. Therefore, applying these research lines to explain changes in asylum and migration policies may present challenges, including::

(1) From a new institutionalism point of view, institutions constrain political actors, so, in our analytical case, how can it be explained that some Member States are taking national responses contrary to EU asylum law?
(2) From a European integration perspective, national governments may overcome established institutional constraints and use EU institutions seemingly in cooperation but for their own interests. Another research question arises as to why do some Member States not want dialogue or cooperation with the EU, instead seeing it as a useless problem-solving institution in security and migration areas?

Having specified these points for future research, one could argue that until the start of the refugee crisis in 2015 (mainly fleeing the conflict in Syria), the new institutionalism and European integration models had been reasonably effective in explaining European asylum policy changes. Nevertheless, the political integration of the EU might have been altered by the emergence of existential threats, as Huysmans (2000) noted that 'some areas of European cooperation can be transformed when a "critical juncture" occurs'. In this regard, this 'critical juncture' led to some scholars also considering other theoretical perspectives as complementary or an alternative explanation in policy change models. When it comes to analysing asylum and migration policy change, and especially EU regulations, public goods and cost-benefit models have been employed in numerous recent research.

With the massive flows of refugees in recent years, and migration treated as an issue of internal security in the EU, some scholars have attempted to understand this phenomenon from different theoretical angles. Public goods models have been shown to be a useful explanatory perspective in exploring international collective-action and free-riding dynamics (Olson

& Zeckhauser, 1966). According to these analyses, the researchers argue that, when it comes to migration policy change, public goods theory may help to explain developments in EU internal security cooperation (see Betts, 2003; Thielemann & Amstrong, 2013). This calls into question the issue of using alternative theoretical models to explain policy change in the European asylum regime when migration is conceived as a matter of internal security in the EU. This may explain some empirical facts such as the opposition of some Eastern European Member States to possible reform of the Dublin Regulation (Trauner, 2016). Future research should be focused on a theoretical development of the public goods model from a political perspective in order to assess an empirical case. Rather than considering public goods and cost-benefit models as substitutive theoretical frameworks of the new institutionalism and European integration theories, these new theoretical approaches should be seen as complementing the 'old' theoretical frames and the new approaches from other social science disciplines that are being taken into consideration in the political sciences arena.

The overview in this introduction reveals that there is a clear division between before and after the refugee crisis of the theoretical approaches in explaining policy changes in asylum and migration areas. On the one hand, in the case of new institutionalism and European integration process models, the literature is primarily institution-centred and focused on which political actor(s)'s actions are institutionalised. On the other hand, public goods and cost-benefit theories are state-centred/rational choice-based, that is, Member States act depending on their own cost-benefit calculations and particular criteria and interests.

Providing humanitarian protection to refugees requires collective efforts and involves the distribution of costs and benefits of refugee (non-) admission among states. While some references to public goods theory were made in past migration studies, its conceptual understanding has been mostly left vague as to what makes refugee protection a public good. The literature on refugee protection as a public good has been built mostly on rational choice (classical economics) assumptions that consider states to employ fact-based, cost-benefit calculations in their policy choices (see Thielemann & Amstrong, 2013, p. 157). This approach neglects *how* states form their preferences and moreover, it fails to explain the variation in responses to refugee emergencies across the countries (e.g., Betts, 2003, Lutz & Portmann, 2022). This project addresses this shortcoming by developing a novel theoretical framework based on the constructivist paradigm to argue that the benefits of refugee protection are socially constructed based on states' identities and norms. To advance the understanding of asylum governance, this book applies this innovative theoretical framework to investigate the costs and benefits incurred by: forced migration. An important element of this project is to make a comparison about how refugees are framed under a humanitarian or security narrative, depending on the construction of costs and benefits through a frame analysis of Polish government politicians' narratives. The more states perceive refugee admission as a threat or burden and the less they identify with the international liberal order and humanitarian values, the less they will consider refugee protection as a collective good providing benefits to them, and subsequently, the less they will contribute to international responsibility-sharing.

While an ever-growing number of refugees are in need of humanitarian protection, national states are limiting their hosting capacities. A growing literature seeks to understand under which conditions states are willing to admit migrants seeking international protection, but no study has concerned so far refugee flows from neighbouring countries in Poland that may have a major impact at the EU level. In addition, this research fills the gap in the literature on migration policies in Central-Eastern Europe as a region in which these Member States do not have significant experience with refugee flows (forced migration, until very recently), but almost solely economic migrants (labour migration). To address this research gap, I propose to combine two distinct theoretical approaches: (1) the collective action theory (economics) and, (2) social constructivism (sociology). Rational choice fails from criticism when it comes to understanding an actor(s)'s construction of choice preferences. This research provides a unique theoretical framework: an understanding of the constructivist nature of the rational choice framework. It does not reject rational-choice premises but seeks to understand how actors construct their perceptions towards the benefits (constructivism) and maximisation of their utilities for the (non-)provision of a public good (rational choice):

(1) As for the former, I argue that the provision of refugee protection provides collective benefits to states globally, such as maintaining public order and international stability, while the costs of provision fall on the individual states that admit refugees. As refugee protection is an international public good, national states are incentivised to free-ride on the protection efforts of other states instead of contributing them-

selves, which results in the international under-provision of refugee protection.
(2) As for social constructivism, I stress the importance of how national stakeholders (e.g., governments) interpret the circumstances and consequences of refugee emergencies. In a state with an identity built on humanitarianism, refugee protection is considered an appropriate response, whereas in a state with an exclusive national identity and nativist norms, refugee deterrence is viewed an appropriate response.

In this interdisciplinary approach, the actions of stakeholders result from a cost-benefit calculation in which both costs and benefits are interpreted in economic terms (e.g., related to labour market participation of immigrants) and political terms (e.g., public security). From my perspective, the most comprehensive and fitting method to explore the contrasting responses of the Polish government to two refugee crises—those stemming from the Middle East and Ukraine—involves an innovative examination of economic and political paradigms.

REFERENCES

Betts, A. (2003). Public goods theory and the provision of refugee protection: The role of the joint-product model in burden-sharing theory. *Journal of Refugee Studies, 16*(3), 274–296.

Ceccorulli, M. (2009). Migration as a security threat: Internal and external dynamics in the European Union. Forum on the Problems of Peace and War, Florence, Working Paper No: 65/09.

Collier, P. (2014). Illegal migration To Europe: What should be done? *Social Europe Journal*. Retrieved March 22, 2023, from https://www.socialeurope.eu/2014/09/illegal-migration/

Huysmans, J. (2000). The European Union and the securitization of migration. *Journal of Common Market Studies, 38*(5), 751–777.

Lavenex, S. (2001). 'The Europeanization of refugee policies: Normative challenges and institutional legacies. *Journal of Common Market Studies, 39*(5), 851–874.

Lutz, P., & Portmann, L. (2022). Why do states admit refugees? A comparative analysis of resettlement policies in OECD countries. *Journal of Ethnic and Migration Studies, 48*(11), 2515–2539.

Olson, M., & Zeckhauser, R. (1966). An economic theory of alliances. *The Review of Economics and Statistics, 48*(3), 266–279.

Selm-Thorburn, J. V. (1998). *Refugee protection in Europe: Lessons of the Yugoslav crisis*. Kluwer Law International.

Thielemann, E. (2003). Between interests and norms: Explaining burden-sharing in the European Union. *Journal of Refugee Studies, 16*(3), 253–273.

Thielemann, E., & Amstrong, C. (2013). Understanding European asylum cooperation under the Schengen/Dublin system: A public goods framework. *European Security, 22*(2), 148–164.

Thompson, C. (2013). Frontiers and threats: Should transnational migration be considered a security issue? *Global Policy Journal*. Retrieved November 09, 2022, from http://www.globalpolicyjournal.com/blog/20/11/2013/frontiers-and-threats should-transnational-migration-be-considered-security-issue

Trauner, F. (2016). Asylum policy: The EU's 'crises' and the looming policy regime failure. *Journal of European Integration, 38*(3), 311–325.

Wanner, P. (2002). Migration rends in Europe, European Population Papers Series No. 7. European Population Committee's working papers series.

Zaun, N. (2017). *EU asylum policies: The power of strong regulating states*. Palgrave Macmillan.

Zincone, G., & Caponio, T. (2006). The multilevel governance of migration. In R. Penninx, M. Berger, & K. Kraal (Eds.), *The dynamics of international migration and settlement in Europe: A state of the art* (IMISCOE Joint Studies Series). Amsterdam University Press.

CHAPTER 2

International Cooperation in Public Goods Provision

INTRODUCTION

Public goods theoretical reasoning has served economists as a catalyst for the understanding of collective action failure in the market context. The initial economics of public goods were analysed by Samuelson in 1954 and 1955. In these two major articles, he showed that the condition for the final contribution of public goods is that the perceived benefits must be greater than the costs. Later on, in 1962, Buchanan and Tullock's inspiring book, *The Calculus of Consent: Logical Foundations of Constitutional Democracy*, set the basis for a theory about collective choice. In 1965, Olson's *The Logic of Collective Action* extended this previous work on public goods provision by adding to the academic debate on procedural theories regarding public goods. Through the analysis of strategic interaction and selective incentives, he showed different types of public goods groups and a hypothesis that smaller groups will succeed at providing public goods better than larger groups where information is diffuse and transaction costs are high (*group size paradox*). One of Olson's major contributions was not just to link collective action and public goods provision, but to give a general idea about how a self-interest approach among the actors may lead to failure in cooperating in certain circumstances and/or situations, especially in politics and international relations. Based on these principles, a considerable amount of literature on public goods interaction has been produced.

© The Author(s), under exclusive license to Springer Nature Switzerland AG 2023
D. Caballero-Vélez, *Contesting Migration Crises in Central Eastern Europe*, Mobility & Politics,
https://doi.org/10.1007/978-3-031-44037-3_2

Most of the cooperation dynamics in politics are dominated by the collective action problem. In academic literature, realists preclude any cooperation between states because of the power self-interest rationale; on the other hand, liberals propose institutions and knowledge as a path to resolve the cooperation problem (Wendt, 1994). Recent literature on public goods provision takes collective action as a reference point in understanding states' cooperation on some political issues such as climate change, migration, peace, and security. States in this sense are organisations that provide public goods for its members, citizens, and other organisations, with provision one of the main functions of any state (Olson, 1965). States' collective behaviour depends on their own incentives and rationale. An individual state will act by its own incentive rather than in the common interest of other states. Thus, in domestic politics, collective failure resulting in the non-provision of public goods is generally addressed by the state; governments must ensure that public goods are provided to citizens. At the international level, states may choose to provide a public good collectively if they are not prepared to provide it unilaterally (Betts, 2009). In international politics, issues such as global security, climate change mitigation, and poverty eradication are considered to be global public goods. If states cannot provide such public goods unilaterally, they engage in and enhance collective action to provide them.

Goods Typology

The characteristics of goods are important to understand how they are perceived by actors. In the case of public goods, they have positive externalities; conversely, if a good does not have externalities, it is not a public good. Goods may be classified according to two criteria: their degree of (a) publicness and (b) globalness. In the first case, depending on the excludability and rivalrous nature of their benefits, goods may be purely public, impurely public, common, club, or private. Recent literature has claimed that globalness may be understood as a dimension of publicness (Kaul, 2008; Kaul et al., 2003): the geographical scope of public goods will depend on the public nature of their benefits. Within the framework of this criteria, benefits may accrue at the global, regional, national, or local level.

Publicness Typology

a. Public goods

In his work, Samuelson (1954, p. 387) emphasises that a public good is one 'which all enjoy in common in the sense that each individual's consumption of such a good leads to no subtracting from any other individual's consumption of that good, thus, the consumption of public good is "joint"'. By implication, public goods are determined by two main characteristics: 'their benefits are non-rivalrous in consumption and non-excludable' (Kaul et al., 1999, p. 3).

It is difficult to find 'pure' public goods as normally, goods are 'impure' by nature, that is, they have mixed benefits: 'as impure goods are more common than the pure type, the term public good is used to encompass both pure and impure public goods' (Kaul et al., 1999, p. 4). Pure public goods are uncommon, and the majority of goods, even those often labeled as public goods, provide benefits to their contributors. (Sandler, 1977). An example of a pure public good would be maintaining international peace, as states contribute to the peace by providing support to international peacekeeping operations in conflict zones and, accordingly, benefits from this provision accrue to all states. Impure public goods or goods that conform to a 'joint product model' (see Sandler, 1977; Sandler & Tschirhart, 1980) provide excludable benefits to the contributors that have provided them. According to this model, by providing a public good, multiple benefits of different 'degree(s) of publicness' arise to different states.

Another important characteristic of public goods is the free-riding problem (characteristic of collective action failure). Public goods' non-excludability leads the supplier of a public good to risk a cost that others benefit from without paying for it. This is a problem that often results in over-exploited or under-produced public goods (Long & Woolley, 2009).

b. Private goods

Private goods are excludable and exclusive in consumption and are associated with property rights, while their use depends on the owners. In addition, in order to obtain the benefits of private goods, individual consumers have to pay for them (Kaul et al., 2003). In the case of private goods, the free-riding problem is avoided.

c. Common goods

It is very often that common goods tend to be confused with public goods. Scholars (see Dupré, 1993; Cahill, 2005) have summarised two important characteristics of common goods: (a) are rival in consumption and (b) required collective action. In opposition to public goods in which collective action is not needed for their provision, common goods cannot be provided by individuals acting by their own alone (Deneulin & Townsend, 2007). Some examples of common goods are ecosystems (e.g., forests) or land-based resources such as mineral deposits. In these cases, wood or minerals collection is only possible through collective action. Despite being publicly available, these goods exhibit rivalry, as consumption by one individual results in a reduction of the overall quantity.

d. Club goods

The concept of a club good has been explained several times in the literature on public goods. Cornes and Sandler (1996, p. 347) identify a club as a 'voluntary group of individuals who derive mutual benefit from sharing one or more of the following: production costs, the members' characteristics, or a good characterised by excludable benefits'. As Sandler and Tschirhart (1980) suggest, the literature on club goods has its roots in Olson's (1965) and Buchanan's (1965) investigations. Olson (1965) claims that clubs share public goods and made a distinction between inclusive and exclusive clubs:

- Inclusive clubs: share public goods without requiring membership.
- Exclusive clubs: share impure public goods and require a restrictive form of membership.

It is important to note that clubs involve sharing, both for the common use of an impure public good and/or its enjoyment by the members of the club (Cornes & Sandler, 1996). This 'sharing' provides the attribution to the club good of being partially rivalrous (Cornes & Sandler, 1996). By acquiring club membership, one receives the good's 'excludability' characteristic (benefits are only consumed by club members). Another important characteristic of club goods is the 'congestion' problem: club goods are 'subject to some rivalry in the form of congestion' (Sandler, 2013, p. 266). This means that when the club good is overconsumed, it may lead to a deterioration of the good's quantity or quality (Sandler, 2013). An example of a club good is the swimming pool of a housing complex, in which its enjoyment is only 'consumed' by the residents of the housing complex and non-rivalrous until congestion occurs; another example is a discount in a cinema in which membership is required to receive those benefits that are excludable from people who are not members of the cinema association.

Globalness Typology

The term 'global' refers not only to geography but also to sociological and temporal dimensions as well (Kaul et al., 1999), in this case, a 'public good that benefits just one country would not be considered global but regional or national' (Kaul et al., 1999, p. 12). In this context, to differentiate between those levels, Kaul and Mendoza (2003) point out that one may focus on 'the scope of the public goods' benefits and the level at which it may be situated or from which its effects may emanate' (p. 107). These scholars give some examples, such as pollution, which can arise locally but spread globally, or development assistance situated at the international level but designed for a regional effect such as support for administrators. Within the framework of these criteria, 'globalness' is considered a dimension of publicness: the more that goods are public in nature, the wider the geographical area their benefits will be spread.

A further point is how different institutions provide different types of public goods. Depending on subsidiarity,[1] public goods are provided by global, regional, and national and/or local institutions (Sandler, 2006). Global institutions supply global public goods, regional institutions, regional public goods, and national governments, national public goods.

a. Global public goods

---

[1] 'Subsidiarity indicates that the decision-making jurisdiction should coincide with a public good's region of spillovers. When the spillover range of the public good extends beyond the political jurisdiction, decision makers often fail to account for all who benefit and, consequently, the public good is undersupplied' (Sandler, 2006, p. 15).

Global or transnational public goods refer to goods whose effects are felt in different states. The two main types of transnational public goods are global and regional, both provide non-rivalrous and non-excludable benefits to the citizens of different countries. Nevertheless, the main difference between these two public goods is rooted in the spillover effect (Sandler, 2006):

- Global public goods provide a benefit or cost spillover at the global level, for example, efforts to reduce ozone-depleting chlorine improve the wellbeing of people worldwide.
- Regional public goods provide benefit or cost spillover to two or more countries in a given location.

These descriptions of global and regional public goods may be confusing as some regional institutions may have spillover to external countries outside of a given location; accordingly, in order to identify properly global and regional public goods, it is crucial to look at the effects, particularly if different, in third countries. States provide global public goods such as international security and peace if the utility gained from the public good is high (Roberts, 2019). At the national level, 'any state committed to solving these issues will be inclined to support co-operative, international efforts designed to address them' (Kelemen, 2010, p. 337).

b. Regional public goods

In the case of regional public goods, where there is less spillover to fewer countries, collective action is likely to succeed. As mentioned above, regional public goods are commonly provided by regional institutions. When a public good is provided by a specific institution, countries in that region will benefit from the public good. When it comes to defining a region, whether geographical, cultural, political, or some other kind, the characteristics determine the extent of the benefits and may influence spillover (Sandler, 2006). When analysing regional public goods, the *aggregation technology* approach,[2] can provide interesting insights into the possible levels of provision (Liu & Kahn, 2017):

---

[2] Sandler (2006) refers to aggregation technology as property that influences the incentives of contributors and, consequently, the final supply.

- Summation—when the total provision level equals the sum of each country's contribution;
- Best shot—the largest country contribution determines the aggregate level;
- Weakest link—the lowest country contribution determines the aggregate level.

Therefore, regional public goods provision needs an institutional agreement to allow efficient coordination. In the absence of regional institutions setting up legally binding norms, very often provision requires voluntary cooperation (Anand, 2002). In terms of 'free-riding', regional public goods may suffer from under-provision if there is not a competent regional institution to provide them. For instance, the lack of integration in EU policy domains might suggest a weak process and, consequently, high chances of not providing a Europe-wide public good (Caballero-Vélez & Pachocka, 2021). Nevertheless, due to the differing degree of competences between the EU and the Member States, it is difficult to determine spillover in regional public goods in the EU.

c. National and local public goods

National public goods are provided by state governments. The main difference between a national and transnational public good (global or regional) is the free-riding problem: in the case of national public goods, there is no free-riding involving other states because there is no spillover (Sandler, 2006). In economic literature, national public goods used to be related to public expenditure: Samuelson established that public goods could only be provided efficiently by taxing the public (Seo, 2016). Recent literature locates national public goods by means other than taxation, for instance, Barrett (2007) analyses the case of clean air as a public good: clean air is a national public good if (1) it is provided by a national government; (2) spillover remains at the national level; (3) there are no other states benefiting from this public good (no free-riding problem).

In the study of national public goods, it is important to point out that individual collective action is needed for the supply of national governments. Although national public goods are supplied by the state, citizens must contribute for there to be a supply; for instance, citizens contribute to street lighting by paying taxes because it is in the common interest. Nevertheless, when it comes to the provision of public goods that stimulates different opinions within the society, some individuals may not contribute and government risks not providing it.

The identification of local public goods is 'primarily because they are typically provided locally and the benefits tend to be local as well' (Batina & Ihori, 2005, p. 3). Some examples of local public goods are sidewalks and traffic lights (Batina & Ihori, 2005). In general, local and national public goods have similar characteristics—non-rivalrous and non-excludable benefits and free-riding is less likely.

GAME THEORY AND 'BURDEN-SHARING' IN PUBLIC GOODS PROVISION

The collective action problem has its roots in the assumption that individuals do not act to achieve common interests but are self-interested, and this leads to situations in which benefits from cooperation are not achieved (see Olson, 1965; Olson & Zeckhauser, 1966). Olson (1965) noted that the free-riding problem is characteristic of all groups except smaller ones. While in small groups the lack of individual participation can lead to collective action failure, in larger groups a few individual participants deciding not to join can go unnoticed, so self-interested organisations and individuals may choose to free-ride unless they are constrained (Heckathorn, 1996). For Olson, a larger group,[3] persuades individuals towards the contribution to the collective good by (a) providing incentives to join the group, (b) punishment and coercion if they do not join the group. By incentivising them to join the group and contribute to the collective good, individuals are motivated by receiving *positive selective incentives* (positive rewards); on the other hand, not contributing to the collective good may lead to *negative selective incentives* in the form of punishment (Olson, 1965).

The idea of sharing the costs of public goods provision in latent groups was first conceived in 1966 by Olson and Zeckhauser in their seminal title, *The Economic Theory of Alliances*. This book explores the contributions to common costs in the case of NATO and how states share alliance defence expenditures. The shift in NATO strategy from deterrence to defence led some scholars to conclude that there are partially rivalrous benefits (see Sandler & Cauley, 1975; Sandler & Forbes, 1980). Contrary to Olson's

---

[3] Those 'groups', called 'latent', refer to ones with major capacity for action; in the case of international defence, NATO, or in political integration, the EU.

pure public benefits postulates by which burden-sharing is needed to avoid collective action failures, the impure nature of the good may lead to different degrees of burden-sharing. Governments are not perfectly rational by nature—they alter their actions' utility on the basis of incomplete goals and information (Simon, 1985) and act mostly to fulfil egoistic objectives (Oneal, 1990).

The alliance collective defence model served to advance the understanding of burden-sharing dynamics in collective action situations. Most collection action situations arise from *social dilemmas* from which scholars have employed game theoretical models to understand them (Heckathorn, 1996): some of them analyse collective action such as the N-Prisoner's Dilemmas with the free-riding problem,[4] others investigate collective action in social interaction terms, and some neglect collective action problems with social dilemmas altogether.

Formal analysis of collective action situations employs rational-choice models (Olson, 1965; Marwell & Pamela, 1993) in which actors act according to an increase in their expectations of receiving a benefit from the contribution. The most representative situation of this kind of collective action is the N-Prisoner's Dilemma. It assumes an *equilibrium of power* between prisoners. The Olsonian collective action model assumes the pureness of a public good, which means a non-contribution still will provide benefits, that is, to free-riders. In the case of the Prisoners' dilemma, this equilibrium of power is an analogy to the pureness of a good, meaning one prisoner will 'free-ride' on the other's action. This model has been applied in order to explain rational-choice dynamics in international cooperation (international relations). On the one hand, it may be useful to explain hegemony in some specific areas in which actors have a symmetrical relation of power and interests; on the other hand, it does not explain collective action failure in every case of international cooperation, as normally not every state has the same power and interests in a given circumstance. Normally, most public goods are impure in nature, which means that actors act in an asymmetrical relationship of power according to their individual incentives.

[4] In 1950, Melvin Dresher and Merrill Flood from the Rand Corporation analysed a number of examples about the equilibrium of non-zero-sum games. Tucker developed a payoff matrix by designing the story about two prisoners when analysing the problem of a non-zero-sum scenario (Straffin, 1993). In Betts' words (2009, p. 28): 'the dilemma is derived from the analogy of two prisoners who have been arrested and accused of a crime but are detained and interrogated separately from one another'.

When it comes to analysing international cooperation, it is very often linked to the *Olsonian* collective action approach, and public goods theory to cooperation between states. The identification of a public good is a political decision. When the good is at the international level, the production process is set by the international regime,[5] and implementation of rules. The likelihood of effective implementation depends on political governments and their cooperation with the international regime and their perceptions of a public good's costs and benefits. International relations (IR) literature identifies global public goods provision as a core element in understanding states' different rationales in enhancing cooperation or not (see Kaul et al., 1999, 2003). Nevertheless, not only can global public goods be considered objects of analysis in cooperation at the international level but also other public goods, such as regional ones, may be situated at the global level. Thus, national public goods 'become transnational-regional or global when they cannot be maintained or improved solely through domestic policy action' (Kaul et al., 2003, p. 331). States may cooperate in the provision of goods at the international level in different ways. Accordingly, Kaul et al. (2003) shows the main forms of international cooperation in the provision of goods: outward-oriented cooperation, inward-oriented cooperation, joint intergovernmental production and networked cooperation. Examples include:

- Outward-oriented cooperation: the rationale for international cooperation is to encourage others, as national public goods are not well-provided or national policies are not enough to provide public goods at the national level. An example of this type of cooperation is promoting financial stability.
- Inward-oriented cooperation: a demand by country 'A' to the rest for cooperation may lead to an international agreement that can be translated into national policy adjustments.
- Joint intergovernmental production: countries that assign the production of a public good to an international organisation. In this case, an example would be global disease surveillance.

---

[5] Directorate-General for Development and International Cooperation and Ministry of Foreign Affairs Treasury Directorate, Ministry of the Economy, Finance and Industry of France. 'Global Public Goods'. Source: https://www.diplomatie.gouv.fr/IMG/pdf/biens_publ_gb.pdf.

- Networked cooperation: a combination of the first two types. International networks require an 'entrance fee' from members; for example, a fee that consists of requirements standardising national policies.

One of the main problems in the field of international cooperation and public goods studies is understanding the states' rationales behind the collective action. Broadly speaking, when it comes to analysing international cooperation through a public goods perspective, it is important to understand state actors' self-interest.

On this subject, Rhinard (2009) claims that international cooperation's main aim should be to provide common solutions to common problems; nevertheless, seeking solutions in a cooperative way is a tough task. The problem of finding common solutions could be explained through analysis of the difficulties in producing a public good through common collective action. On this point, the public goods approach helps confirm that solutions are at the national level (Rhinard, 2009); in other words: 'solutions to public goods problems come in the form of a delegation to a third party with enforcement power: the government' (Rhinard, 2009, p. 444).

In the case of the form of joint intergovernmental production, international organisations are the main actors providing global public goods nowadays and are central actors in international politics (Carbone, 2007). Accordingly, public goods theory and, specifically, the provision of global public goods, is used by scholars in order to understand international cooperation among states. The provision of global public goods through international organisations (e.g., UN, World Bank), show states´ attitudes behind their rationales. When an international organisation provides a global public good, members of that organisation (states) may contribute towards the good's provision, so the contribution is operationalised in the form of cooperation. Based on Samuelson's economic approach to public goods, 'if politicians are viewed as competitive suppliers of public and other goods and services and their voters as consumers of these goods and services, it cannot be surprising that politicians are tempted to collude' (Vaubel, 1986, p. 44) or, in other words, to free-ride.

In the case of EU public goods provision, it takes the form of joint intergovernmental production. Due to the complexity of the EU policy-making (shared competences with Member States), the production of public goods must be analysed by looking at the specific policy domain and its shared competences. In the case of an international organisation like the EU, countries assign it to provide a global public good; in the case of the EU, when Member States are interested in contributing to the provision of public goods (normally by transferring competences to the EU), the EU, by setting up legal norms, provides regional public goods with spillovers to all Member States, which leads some of them to free ride.

Conclusions

This chapter has addressed the question of whether the collective action problem is a social dilemma. Since Olson's foundational model (1965), there have been few attempts to understand the provisioning of public goods in collective action failures. Olson and Zeckhauser's (1966) seminal article was groundbreaking for its understanding of burden-sharing in collective action scenarios. While Olson clearly specified the pureness of public goods and the consequences in terms of free-riding dynamics, other authors have advanced our knowledge of burden-sharing by applying game theoretical models.

We can draw a series of implications from these insights for the understanding of burden-sharing in public goods provision and international cooperation among states. Firstly, to comprehend the extent to which actors can engage in free-riding within a collective action scenario, it is essential to grasp the concept of the public nature inherent in public goods. The nature of public goods (local, national, regional, and global) is likely to be multi-dimensional and provide benefits of different degrees of publicness (impure). Secondly, actors' interactions lead to social dilemmas and collective action failure scenarios that may be analysed through game theoretical models. Depending on the type of good, these models may be used for different outcomes, but most likely they will show us strategic interactions in burden-sharing between individuals. Last but not least, collective action logic is embedded in the international cooperation between states. States act following their own self-interests, leading them to cooperate or not on certain issues. In latent groups, larger states may use coercive means or incentives to motivate smaller states to cooperate in order to avoid free-riding. In medium-size groups, states will cooperate if others do the same, although a lack of cooperation in these situations is likely to occur.

REFERENCES

Anand, P. B. (2002). Financing the provision of global public goods. UNU/ WIDER Discussion Paper No. 2002/110. Retrieved January 20, 2023, from https://archive.unu.edu/hq/library/Collection/PDF_files/WIDER/ WIDERdp2002.110.pdf
Batina, R. G., & Ihori, T. (2005). *Public goods: Theories and evidences.* Springer.
Barrett, S. (2007). *Why Cooperate? The Incentive to Supply Global Public Goods.* Oxford: Oxford University Press.
Betts, A. (2009). *Protection by persuasion: International cooperation in the refugee regime.* Cornell University Press.
Buchanan, J. M. (1965). An economic theory of clubs. *Economica, 32*, 1–14.
Caballero-Vélez, D., & Pachocka, M. (2021). Producing public goods in the EU: European integration processes in the fields of refugee protection and climate stability. *European Politics and Society, 22*(1), 1–18.
Cahill, L. (2005). Globalization and the Common Good. In J. A. Coleman, W. F. Ryan, & B. Ryan (Eds.), *Globalization and catholic social thought: Present crisis, future hope* (pp. 42–54). Orbis Books.
Carbone, M. (2007). Supporting or resisting global public goods. *Global Governance, 13*(2), 179–198.
Cornes, R., & Sandler, T. (1996). *The theory of externalities, public goods, and club goods.* Cambridge University Press.
Deneulin, S., & Townsend, N. (2007). Public goods, global public goods and the common good. *International Journal of Social Economics, 34*(1–2), 19–36.
Dupré, L. (1993). The common good and the open society. *The Review of Politics, 55*(4), 687–712.
Heckathorn, D. D. (1996). The dynamics and dilemmas of collective action. *American Sociological Review, 61*(2), 250–277.
Kaul, I. (2008). Providing (contested) global public goods. In V. Rittberger, M. Nettesheim, & C. Huckel (Eds.), *Authority in the global political economy* (International Political Economy Series) (pp. 89–115). Palgrave Macmillan.
Kaul, I., Conceição, P., Le Goulven, K., & Mendoza, R. U. (2003). Why do global public goods Matter Today? In P. C. Kaul, K. Le Goulven, & R. U. Mendoza (Eds.), *Providing global public goods: Managing globalization* (pp. 2–20). Oxford University Press.
Kaul, I., Grunberg, I., & Stern, M. A. (1999). *Global public goods: International cooperation in the 21st Century.* Oxford University Press.
Kaul, I., & Mendoza, R. U. (2003). Advancing the concept of public goods. In I. Kaul, P. Conceição, K. Le Goulven, & R. U. Mendoza (Eds.), *Providing*

global public goods: Managing globalization (pp. 78–111). Oxford University Press.

Kelemen, R. D. (2010). Globalizing European Union environmental policy. *Journal of European Public Policy, 17*(3), 335–349.

Liu, T., & Kahn, T. (2017). Regional public goods cooperation: An inductive approach to measuring regional public goods. In A. Estevadeordal & L. W. Goodman (Eds.), *21st Century cooperation: Regional public goods, global governance, and sustainable development* (pp. 14–36). Routledge.

Long, D., & Woolley, F. (2009). Global public goods: Critique of a UN discourse. *Global Governance, 15*(1), 107–122.

Marwell, G., & Pamela, O. (1993). *The critical mass in collective action: A micro-social theory.* Cambridge University Press.

Olson, M. (1965). *The logic of collective action. Public goods and the theory of groups.* Harvard University Press.

Olson, M., & Zeckhauser, R. (1966). An economic theory of alliances. *The Review of Economics and Statistics, 48*(3), 266–279.

Oneal, J. R. (1990). The theory of collective action and burden sharing in NATO. *International Organization, 44*(3), 379–402.

Rhinard, M. (2009). European cooperation on future crises: Toward a public good? *Review of Policy Research, 26*(4), 439–455.

Roberts, J. C. (2019). *Constructing global public goods.* Lexington Books.

Samuelson, P. A. (1954). The pure theory of public expenditures. *Review of Economics and Statistics, 36*(4), 350–356.

Samuelson, P. A. (1955). Diagrammatic exposition of a theory of public expenditure. *The Review of Economics and Statistics, 37*(4), 350–356.

Sandler, T. (1977). Impurity of defence: An application of the economics of alliances. *Kyklos, 30*(3), 443–460.

Sandler, T. (2006). Regional public goods and international organizations. *The Review of International Organization, 1*(1), 5–25.

Sandler, T. (2013). Buchanan clubs. *Constitutional Political Economy, 24*(4), 265–284.

Sandler, T., & Cauley, J. (1975). On the economic theory of alliances. *Journal of Conflict Resolution, 19*(2), 330–348.

Sandler, T., & Forbes, J. F. (1980). Burden-sharing, strategy and the design of NATO. *Economic Enquiry, 18*(2), 425–444.

Sandler, T., & Tschirhart, J. T. (1980). The economic theory of clubs: An evaluative survey. *Journal of Economic Literature, 18*(4), 1481–1521.

Seo, S. N. (2016). A theory of global public goods and their provisions. *Journal of Public Affairs, 16*(4), 394–405.

Simon, H. A. (1985). *Models of bounded rationality.: Economic analysis and public policy.* MIT Press.
Straffin, P. D. (1993). *Game Theory and Strategy* (1st ed., Vol. 36). Mathematical Association of America.
Vaubel, R. (1986). A public choice approach to international organization. *Public Choice, 51*(1), 39–57.
Wendt, A. (1994). Collective identity formation and the international state. *The American Political Science Review, 88*(2), 384–396.

CHAPTER 3

Constructing Public Goods: Actors' Rationales Behind Actions

INTRODUCTION

Rationale in public goods theory has its origins in the public finance dichotomy tradition between the normative and positivist approaches (see Buchanan, 1968/1999; Musgrave, 1959; Samuelson, 1954). Individuals are interpreted to be fully rational decision-making units that act in an attempt to reach the optimal outcome (Buchanan & Tullock, 1962, p. 213). The 'classical' literature on public goods theory set the roots of the rational choice model as a way to understand public goods production. Rational choice focuses purely on actors' instrumental actions, within the objectives as given, therefore, not in the formation of these objectives; in other words, the theoretical approach is not interested in answering how actors reach their objectives (Popa, 2015). Rational choice theory has been understood through the lens of positivist hermeneutics. It has its origins in the economic theory in which assumptions about human behaviour are based on the maximisation of utility (Buchanan & Tullock, 1962/1999). As a result, individuals make their choices according to the expected benefits that are to be provided by each decision.

Rational choice fails criticism when it comes to providing a general idea about actors' choices (Goode, 1997). While rational choice may give interesting insight into an individual's rationale in determining choices, its mathematical method of analysis cannot fully explain human behaviour. It

© The Author(s), under exclusive license to Springer Nature Switzerland AG 2023
D. Caballero-Vélez, *Contesting Migration Crises in Central Eastern Europe*, Mobility & Politics,
https://doi.org/10.1007/978-3-031-44037-3_3

does not take into account social interactions, situations, and so on, and human behaviour might not be analysed without considering all these elements. The following section shows how, on the one hand, rational choice has been used to explain individuals' choices in providing public goods, and, on the other hand, how alternative theoretical models such as constructivism, may be useful in analysing actors' decisions in the provision of public goods. In order to overcome these shortcomings, there have been attempts to understand public goods provision by analysing how social interactions may influence actors' preferences on public goods (see Kaul & Mendoza, 2003; Roberts, 2019). This chapter seeks to provide a constructivist understanding of public goods' provision by analysing how actors construct their preferences in a situation of collective action. This approach is not instrumentalist itself and does not focus on the action by maximising benefits utility, but seeks to explain the preferences behind the different choices: benefits and costs are social constructions and, subsequently, perceived in a different way among actors. The intention is not to reject rational choice premises in public goods provision dynamics but to provide insights about the constructivist nature of the rational choice approach itself.

Maximising Benefits: Rational Choice Reasoning

In the classical approach to rational choice, the psychological interpretation of the theory is used to explain what motivates thought and action. This interpretation, commonly referred to as the 'internalist interpretation' of rational-choice theory, claims that mental entities (the preferences and beliefs) of individuals are related directly with choice (Satz & Ferejohn, 1994). According to this assumption, for an individual's every choice, we may inquire as to the casual relation with the agent's preferences and beliefs. This raises many questions about whether the 'internalist interpretation' can accurately be used to explain cases employed in certain social sciences fields such as political science, in which a psychological approach cannot explain some phenomena. After Von Neumann and Morgenstern postulated their utility theorem of rational behaviour in his classic book, *Theory of Games and Economic Behavior* (1944), in which the utility calculus model is introduced to explain actors' decisions of choices, rational choice theorists started to investigate individuals' rational behaviour in terms of gains and losses.

Economics is embedded in the real world, and prominent scholars such as Schumpeter (1943) and Buchanan and Tullock (1962) sought to explain the economics innate in individuals' choices and actions by assuming that (political) agents/individuals behave in a similar way as markets do.[1] Based on this rationale, public choice theory assumes that individuals are rational and 'behave as if they engage in a cost-benefit analysis of each and every choice available to them before plumping for the option most likely to maximise a given utility function' (Hay, 2004, p. 41). In the context of agents' decision on making choices, rational choice theory assumes a logic of consequences in which preferences are given by the agent's individual utility.[2] Thus, rational choice theorists do not look at the source of utility that determines preferences (Roberts, 2019), in other words, it analyses the *how* but not the *why*.

Jeremy Bentham (1823, p. 2) defines utility as 'the property of an action, a thought, an outcome, or an event that creates satisfaction, benefit, advantage, pleasure, or good in an agent'. Although there are many definitions of utility in public choice theory, the one developed by Bentham has been widely claimed to be one of the richest in content. On this subject, Roberts (2019) explores Bentham's concept and makes an interesting classification of utility into 'dimensions':

(1) *Individual dimension:* reflects the 'agent's idiosyncratic tastes that are experienced and biological responses to stimuli' (p. 16). This dimension refers to the agents' preferences based on past experiences. Rational choice theory claims that this dimension of utility is the one that determines the preferences that lead to the final choice, for instance, a person who does not eat chocolate because they do not like the flavour or texture, or there is some trauma related to an experience from childhood, or simply does not know why. In this dimension, psychology and neuroscience play a crucial role in understanding the utility motivation(s).
(2) *Social dimension:* refers to 'what the agent believes and understands is appropriate to desire in the situation of choice' (p. 17). This

---

[1] Agents are considered the subjects or individuals that carry on an action in a social situation. In political science, it may be defined as any actor that plays a role in a political situation (e.g., states, institutions, governments, NGOs, etc.).
[2] Rational choice theorists assume that preferences are stable and agents' choices are determined by preferences learned in the past (Roberts, 2019).

dimension involves social interactions/structures that constrain an agent's preferences when making choices. March and Olsen (1989) called references to this utility action the 'logic of appropriateness'.[3] Utility in the social dimension involves an assessment of the norms and rules by which the agent has developed their own identity, which determines utility and preferences. The agent's behaviour is a product of the result of this identity framed by and constructed around social structures. Therefore, agents behave according to their own constructed identity, which leads to the formation of preferences (see Diagram 3.1).

Rational choice theory focuses mainly on the first dimension of utility. It does not take into account why agents have different preferences in a given situation, rather it explains the action process. In this regard, rational choice theorists see the action process as a consequence of facts: individuals are rational if they are instrumentally rational, and they are instrumentally rational if they have a preference-ordering system (Hindmoor, 2006, p. 184).

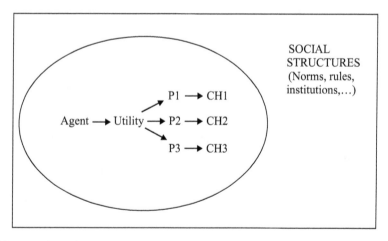

Diagram 3.1 Agent's action process. (Source: Own elaboration)

[3] The 'logic of appropriateness refers' to 'action [that] involves evoking an identity or role and matching the obligations of that identity or role to a specific situation' (March & Olsen, 1989, p. 951).

Diagram 3.1 shows how the agent must select from Choice 1 (CH1), Choice 2 (CH2), and Choice 3 (CH3) according to which preference (P1; P2; P3) maximises the most utility. To illustrate it further, it is helpful to introduce and discuss an imaginary case in which an individual preference for whether to eat lamb, beef, or pork will always be pork. The individual in question is located in a Muslim country that, despite its norms and rules, provides pork for foreigners in selected restaurants. Although the individual's main preference may be to eat pork, in a Muslim country, the person is socially constrained to choose another type of meat instead of pork as it is not typically visible (available), so the individual's choice is beef. In this case, rational choice does not explain *why* the individual prefers beef rather than pork but examines the process itself: the individual chose beef rather than pork or lamb because in this scenario, the utility is maximised—more benefits than costs. Rational choice theorists would not focus on justifying the decision of choosing beef but show how utility is maximised by that choice.

Rational choice theorists may argue that the agent chose beef to eat because of some past experiences that shaped the person's preferences, such as taste, texture, and so on; they would not examine social constraints about eating pork in a Muslim country. Constructivist theorists claim that reality is socially constructed—the main events in society are interpreted through the construction of social beliefs. Subsequently, actors' choices are driven by perceptions and interpretations of beliefs, that is, the actors ask themselves *why* when making specific choices—the selection of action is questioned. The next section more deeply reviews the constructivist theoretical approach for a better understanding of the nature of agents' preferences in making choices and the subsequent provision of public goods.

A Heuristic Alternative: Constructivist Reasoning

Historically, in the political sciences field, rational choice and constructivist theorists have been expanding on numerous debates about the best approach to analysis in the public choice field. Rational-choice scholars have been deeply criticised in ontological terms; the fact that individuals behave by aggregation level models with no consideration of the external environment has found strong opposition in constructivists. On the other side, constructivism has been criticised for lacking the empirical resources of observational experience of the world. Constructivism assumes that rules are built by people's own beliefs. For constructivists, reality determines an individual's behaviour and, consequently, the perception of utility. It seeks to explain the *why* of the choice selected, and not the *how* of the process of action itself.

By the same token, the agents' utility and preferences are constructed by their identities (Roberts, 2016, 2019; Wendt, 1987, 1994): in the process of action, individuals are moved by *utility-identity* behaviour. The study of identity in international relations literature (see Berger, 1966; Onuf, 1989; Wendt, 1992, 1994, 1999) has barely attempted to explain the role of identity in the utility rationale of the actors' choices. The initial and 'few' attempts to overcome the lack of evidence of the identity-utility approach include Weinstein and Deutchberger's famous concept of 'altercasting'. In their outstanding contribution, *Some Dimensions of Altercasting* (1963), Weinstein and Deutschberger define 'altercasting' as 'projecting an identity, to be assumed by other(s) with whom one is in interaction, which is congruent with one's own goals' (1963, p. 454). Weinstein and Deutschberger's work focused initially merely on 'interpersonal control', an example of which would be the U.S.-USSR relationship during the Cold War.[4] In recent years, additional development of this explanation comes from other scholars seeking to explain states' identity formation by identifying the 'others' in security terms (see Campbell, 1988; Kubálková, 2001) and to explain agents' motivations to act (Risse, 2000; Roberts, 2016, 2019). From a state-centred perspective, a government's own identity shapes its vision of reality and determines the norms to establish what is appropriate, followed by formulating policies according to it.

The case in Diagram 3.2 under a constructivist analysis will lead us to argue that the individual 'prefers' to eat beef because it was the 'most appropriate' thing to do when in a Muslim country. Rules and customs constrain individual's utility, preferences, and, consequently, choice. In choosing beef, the individual's utility is maximised not because of preference, for example, taste, but because of societal pressure in the country. According to March and Olsen (1989), decisions are ruled by 'what is appropriate' and actions are 'institutionalised'. If an individual's actions are institutionalised and contrary to their own individual 'logic of appropriateness' rationale, then there is a conflict between what is appropriate for the individual and what is appropriate given the institutional/social

---

[4] Neumann (1999) exemplifies the U.S.-USSR mutual 'othering' as a demonetisation identification process for controlling the other.

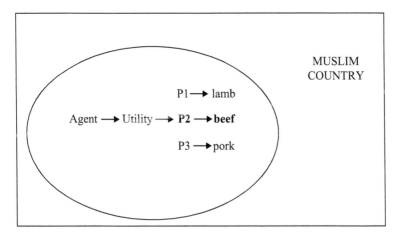

Diagram 3.2 Case 1. (Source: Own elaboration)

structure. While this new institutionalism and rational choice differ in many aspects, they have in common an important factor: rational behaviour. New institutionalists assume that individual behaviour is constrained by institutions in which processes are important, while rational choice theorists maintain the individualist approach within a utility maximisation model in which outcomes are more important than processes. On the contrary, Roberts (2016) assumes that preferences are rules, and may be defined as 'social rules' that are preceded by the agent's identity. Even if to some extent institutional rules may influence agents' actions, in situations of 'critical junctures', the agents' norms (preferences) prevail to the institutions' rules. Contrary to the rational choice utility maximising behaviour, the constructivist approach in explaining public goods provision explains actors' construction of identity (see Roberts, 2019).

The Identity-Utility Model

This model, which seems to be ages old, is the study of how identity shapes individuals' choices. However, it was only recently that scholars sought to provide a constructivist-identity approach to explain the provision of public goods (see Roberts, 2019). In order to synthesise how identity affects choice, Roberts (2019, p. 24) gives three steps:

(1) The identity of the agent relative to the other agents in the situation of choice must be established;
(2) Then, the interests (utilities) generated by that identity must be catalogued;
(3) Finally, the effect of the utilities on preferences and choice must be derived.

Although social contexts are analysed together as one of the main factors that may influence the construction of identities and the individual decision-making process, recently, some scholars have taken an economic approach to explain the role of identity in individuals' choices (see Akerlof & Kranton, 2000; Costa-i-Font & Cowell, 2015). These attempts to 'rationalise' identity in a maximising-benefits-calculus model originated as opposition to the constructivist identity-utility model. Akerlof and Kranton (2005) assumes that if identity captures a person's self-image, in a model of utility, identity describes the gains and losses in utility from behaviour formed by the norms of certain social categories in specific contexts. For that reason, Akerlof and Kranton (2000) argue that identity is based on actions, prescriptions, and categories, in which prescriptions are the norms, beliefs, and rules inherent in each category. According to Akerlof and Kranton (2000), an individual's utility (U_j) may be modelled as follows:

$$U_j = U_j\left(a_j, a_{-j}, I_j\right)$$

In which a_j refers to the action of j, and a_{-j} refers to the actions of other actors. Taking into consideration this model, Akerlof and Kranton (2000) operationalise the individual's identity as follows:

$$I_j = I_j\left(a_j, a_{-j}, c_j, P\right)$$

In this case, P refers to prescriptions (ideas and beliefs assumed by the individual) and c_j refers to social categories, such as group, one of the social categories an individual may be identified with. Therefore, in utility function terms, an individual identity gains when the individual belongs to a group, so the individual mainly focuses on groups with the most favourable benefits in a certain situation (Wichardt, 2008). Identification with the determined group shapes, to some extent, the individual's identity, choices, and preferences. A static economic model of identity based on the sum of preferences fails to explain in detail the choice process. This calculus of building identity by quantifying benefits may provide interesting insights about how other variables, such as group preference, may play an important role in individuals' final choice, but it cannot fully explain the converse of how identity determines individuals' preferences, as they are social constructions. One of the primary reasons for this is that, empirically, it cannot be made through a quantifiable analysis, but an interpretative one.

In utility function terms, individual identity gains in utility when it belongs to a group—the individual focuses on groups with the most favourable comparisons and a certain situation (Wichardt, 2008). For Keohane (1984), collective interactions in a group have an empathetic nature rather than merely instrumental. Following this line of research, this investigation takes Wendt's approach to collective identity formation (1994) about the assumption that states acquire collective interests through process at the systemic level (democratic institutions, welfare state, and consumerism).

Part of the literature on collective identity is focused on the identity formation process by tracing actors' relationships with others (see Campbell, 1988; Neumann, 1999; Simmel, 1950). In collective identity terms, identifying 'the stranger' can be an important element of the group itself, crucial for self-identification (Simmel, 1950). If we correlate identification of 'others' as an important part of a group's identity formation, we see how its actions are shaped by portraying the image of the 'others' (altercasting) (Diagram 3.3):

Diagram 3.3 Altercasting process. (Source: Own elaboration)

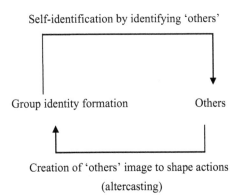

This process leads to the creation of an image of the 'other' that may not correspond with reality, but serves the group as a 'justification' for enhancing certain actions. Altercasting does not refer to the identity formation itself but to how states' actions are shaped depending on the states' self-perception of 'others', that is, 'altercasting' may be considered a utilitarian process in states' identity formation.

Collective Action Failure Paradox

Olson's contribution (1965), based on Pareto's efficiency premise,[5] claimed that, in the case of smaller groups, the likelihood of the provision of the final public good is higher. In collective interaction terms, the group-size-paradox rationale relies on a systemic strategy of interaction based on an exchange of prices to explain behaviour (Stigler & Becker, 1977). The Olsonian group interaction rationality might be represented by Jeffrey Legro's 'two-step process' (1996): (1) preferences are created outside of interaction; (2) interaction shapes actors' behaviour. For a better understanding of the *problèmatique*, I index the group size paradox in a formula in which we assume that two states, w and z, comprise a group, and that a third state, y, joins it. According to the group-size paradox, the final provision will be more difficult to reach because the benefits for each may differ more significantly:

Group size paradox scenario :

$$U_g\left(U_w\left(B^w_1 + B^w_2 + \ldots, B^w_n\right) \approx U_z\left(B^z_1 + B^z_2 + \ldots, B^z_n\right)\right) \neq U_y\left(B^y_1 + B^y_2 + \ldots, B^y_n\right)$$

---

[5] '"Pareto optimality" is an analytical tool for assessing social welfare and resource allocation developed by Italian economist Vilfredo Pareto (1848–1923). Two varieties of Pareto optimality are recognised: strong Pareto optimality (SPO) and weak Pareto optimality (WPO). With SPO, any change will make at least one party worse off. With WPO, any change will make at least one party no better off, but may not make any party worse off. Thus, any SPO situation is also WPO, but not every WPO situation is also SPO. In other words, a SPO situation is "optimal" in the strong sense that any change would make matters worse, at least for someone, whereas a WPO situation is "optimal" in the weaker sense that a change may fail to make the situation better for everyone' (Mock, 2011, p. 808).

3 CONSTRUCTING PUBLIC GOODS: ACTORS' RATIONALES BEHIND ACTIONS   37

The utility of the original group of w and z (U_g) will differ from the utility of the new member of the group (U_y), as the perceived benefits differ from each other. As we see in the formula, collective action is more likely to happen with fewer members interacting. The group-size paradox might be considered an ontological premise with the same maximising-utility framework: the more members in a group, the less likely it will succeed in cooperating. While providing public goods, under a rational choice approach an agent's action may be formulated by a maximising-utility calculus model: rational choice assumes that an agent will enhance action A rather than actions B or C because in a cost-benefit calculus, action A offers the maximised utility (Popa, 2015). If we index this rational-maximising utility premise in a formula, it could be as follows:

$$U^j = X^i \left(\left(B^x_1 + B^x_2 + \ldots, B^x_n \right) > \left(C^x_1 + C^x_2 + \ldots, C^x_n \right) \right)$$

Individuals (agents), indexed by j, maximise their utility (u) by the sum of the public good's benefits (B^x_n) if higher than the sum of the public good's costs (C^x_n). Accordingly, the individual's contribution to the public good's provision (X_n) reads as follows:

$$X_n = J_n \left(u^i \right)$$

The public good, indexed by X_n, is provided by the individual's (J_n) utility-maximising behaviour (u^i). If we transfer this operationalisation in a collective action situation, actors will provide the collective good if the benefits are higher than the costs; nevertheless, some actors may perceive more costs than benefits in the proposed public good provision and may choose not to cooperate. In addition, some agents may act as free-riders and benefit from others' provision contribution. Within the framework of this logic, individuals' utility is maximised by the sum of benefits in choosing a determined action. If we apply this formula to Case 1, it reads as follows:

$$U^j = CH2^i \left(\left(B^x_1 + B^x_2 + \ldots, B^x_n \right) > \left(C^x_1 + C^x_2 + \ldots, C^x_n \right) \right)$$

Here, it shows how the utility of an individual (U^j) is maximised by choosing eating beef (CH2)—there are more benefits than costs.

Table 3.1 Characteristics of rational choice and constructivism in public goods provision

Characteristics	Rational choice	Constructivism
Epistemological nature	Positivist/normative	Social interactions
Utility rationale	Cost/benefit maximising- utility rationale (the *how*)	Identity-utility rationale (the *why*)
Empirical formula	Observable experiences of individuals	Social construction of preferences
Collective action rationale	More benefits than costs	Perceptions of benefits and costs

Source: Own elaboration

Nevertheless, as noted earlier, the rational choice model does not concern itself with the *why* of the individual's decision to eat beef rather than other kind of meat. When it comes to the provision of state-level public goods, as far as interests and norms are part of the state's identity, those interests may give insights about the different norms used in providing public goods (Betts, 2003). In this regard, Table 3.1 shows the main differences in actors' public goods provision rationales in both the rational choice and constructivist approaches:

Classical economics theorists tend to assume that individuals of a group with common interests will act to enhance a common action. If individuals' rationales in a single action derive from utility-maximisation behaviour, in order to enhance collective action, those individuals must be motivated moved by cost-minimisation behaviour (Buchanan & Tullock, 1962). From a purely positivist economic perspective, collective action may be calculated on the basis of 'maximising benefits' and 'minimising costs'. Non-provision of the public good is likely to happen when the group size is higher because:

(a) Individuals will receive fewer benefits;
(b) There are more actors, so the probability of free-riding increases.

In constructivist terms, Betts (2003, p. 287) points out that 'benefits are interpreted according to inter-subjective norms within a given society. As such, a state's desire to protect rights-based norms will directly influence its own perceived 'benefits' from provision'. Those norms forming the perceptions of costs and benefits are based on how appropriate it is to act (logic of appropriateness). This norm-based logic of the appropriateness of action results in divergences between states deciding whether to contribute to the provision of a public good. In the international context, one may argue that a state, before contributing, reflects about the costs and benefits of the provision of the public good, and those perceptions reflect the state's constructed identity, which, at the same time, is based in and also establishes some rules and norms of behaviour (appropriateness). In a group of states, there will be divergences in the perceptions of costs and benefits, typically resulting in a collective-action-failure situation. In contrast to Olson's group-size premise, the number of members is not a crucial factor that reveals the potential degree of cooperation to provide the public good—while there may be bigger groups, the divergences between the member states' perceived benefits are less; or, the opposite, there can be small groups in which collective action failure is guaranteed because there are more divergences between the participants.

States also may perceive benefits and costs in the same way, but change their preferences to maximise utility. This is well-illustrated in the case of the 2003 invasion of Iraq, which divided EU countries. Some of them, including Spain and the UK, supported the U.S.-led military coalition's intervention; others, including Germany and France, did not. If we consider collective security as prevention (deterrence) as a public good (see Roberts, 2019), one may argue that the UK, Spain, and the U.S. perceived the invasion as a necessary action to provide collective security. These countries preferred to act in that way as is maximised utility. In applying a constructivist analysis, we conclude that these states acted to gain some benefits in the form of international prestige and an increase in power or security or both. The following diagram represents an attempt to identify possible motivations (costs/benefits) for action in the form of the military intervention in Iraq:

Diagram 3.4 shows how France preferred not to engage (enhance action) in military intervention during the Iraq invasion. One may notice that France's perceived utility increases without engaging in military intervention, as the benefits of this choice (action) are higher than its costs. The French government's sum of benefits led to the choice of not participating in the military intervention, but it does not explain how this preference was constructed. From an identity-utility model, it would be interesting to examine the French government's self-identity (ideology, U.S.-relationship, role in the EU, etc.), to see to what extent it was crucial

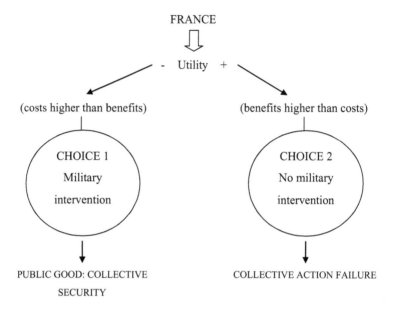

Diagram 3.4 The provision of international security as a public good. (Source: Own elaboration)

in the formation of the preference. For the French government, collective security in this situation was not interpreted as a public good, so in the basic definition its choice would not have contributed to collective action failure between the states. Nevertheless, as the military alliance contained several states, the final public good (according to them) *was* provided. In other words, public goods are socially constructed by agents depending on the perceived maximisation of utility.

In order to develop empirical analysis of this research, the three-step process (Roberts, 2019, p. 24) is a method by which the preferences to the provision of public goods are determined by the agent's self-identity, which, in the first two steps, requires that:

1. The agent's identity in a situation of choice must be established;
2. The interests (utilities) generated by that identity must be catalogued.

The third step is the interpretation of interests in a public good provision situation, so, how the costs and benefits are perceived by the agent.

By applying this identity-utility methodological model, the agents' preferences for the provision of a specific public good become clear.

CONCLUSIONS

This chapter has demonstrated how the nature of public goods is socially constructed by states through their perceptions and practice of norms and customs. States' maximisation of utility relies upon their self-identities, and their perceptions of the costs and benefits of provision of a public good may vary within the group of states. Literature on public goods interactions has not provided detailed explanations about individual's decisions whether to contribute to the final public good. In the collective analysis of members' interaction in a group, the literature focuses on examining a static calculus of the costs and benefits to explain the degree of collective success in providing public goods; nevertheless, the rationalist theoretical approach lacks insights about real individuals' incentives to provide public goods.

The recent scholarship that brings a constructivist framework into rational choice explanations for public goods provision and collective-action failure scenarios (see Kaul & Mendoza, 2003; Roberts, 2019) serves as a catalyst for future investigation of the constructed nature of public goods. Public goods are social constructions determined by rules, norms, and customs that also constitute states' identities. Broadly speaking, public goods come only into existence when states perceive an increase in utility sufficient to contribute to their provision. By understanding the constructed nature of public goods, we may draw insights from the latter, strategic benefit-maximisation interaction process in states' public goods (non-) provision.

The identity-utility model provides useful insights into understanding individuals' preferences for the provision of public goods (and also at the collective level). From an individual perspective, actors *altercast* other actors' identities to try to maximise utility and provide public goods. They behave according to customs and norms based on a logic of appropriateness that define their identities. At the collective level, actors' identities will conform to the identity of the group, influencing the ultimate collective utility. The degree of identity with the collective group depends on the individual degree of identity of each member. Accordingly, if the group's collective identity is weak, the provision of collective public goods will be less likely to happen. The Olsonian static rationale group-size paradox is not rejected, but complemented with an identity-utility constructivist vision of group interactions. Also, if the collective identity is strong, members' divergences in altercasting other actors' identities will decrease.

REFERENCES

Akerlof, G. A., & Kranton, R. E. (2000). Economics and identity. *The Quarterly Journal of Economics, 115*(3), 715–753.
Akerlof, G. A., & Kranton, R. E. (2005). Identity and the Economics of Organizations. *The Journal of Economic Perspectives, 19*(1), 9–32.
Bentham, J. (1823). *An introduction to the principles of morals and legislation.* Clarendon Press.
Berger, P. (1966). Identity as a problem in the sociology of knowledge. *European Journal of Sociology, 7*(1), 32–40.
Betts, A. (2003). Public goods theory and the provision of refugee protection: the role of the joint-product model in burden-sharing theory. *Journal of Refugee Studies, 16*(3), 274–296.
Buchanan, J. M. (1968/1999). *The demand and supply of public goods* (Vol. 5). Liberty Fund. The Collected Works of James M. Buchanan
Buchanan, J. M., & Tullock, G. (1962/1999). *The calculus of consent: logical foundations of constitutional democracy* (Vol. 3). Liberty Fund. The Collected Works of James M. Buchanan.
Campbell, D. (1988). *Writing security: United States foreign policy and the politics of identity* (Revised Edn). University of Minnesota Press.
Costa-i-Font, J., & Cowell, F. (2015). Social Identity and Redistributive Preferences: A Survey. *Journal of Economic Surveys, 29*(2), 357–374.
Goode, W. J. (1997). Rational choice theory. *The American Sociologist, 28*(2), 22–41.
Hay, C. (2004). Theory, stylized heuristic or self-fulfilling prophecy? The status of rational choice theory in public administration. *Public Administration, 62*(1), 39–62.
Hindmoor, A. (2006). *Rational choice.* Palgrave Macmillan.
Kaul, I., & Mendoza, R. U. (2003). Advancing the concept of public goods. In I. Kaul, P. Conceição, K. Le Goulven, & R. U. Mendoza (Eds.), *Providing global public goods: managing globalization* (pp. 78–111). Oxford University Press.
Keohane, R. O. (1984). *After hegemony: cooperation and discord in the world political economy.* Princeton University Press.
Kubálková, V. (2001). Foreign policy, international politics, and constructivism. In V. Kubálková (Ed.), *Foreign policy in a constructed world* (pp. 15–37). M.E. Sharpe.
Legro, J. (1996). Culture and preferences in the international cooperation two-step. *American Political Science Review, 90*(1), 118–137.

March, J. G., & Olsen, J. P. (1989). *Rediscovering Institutions*. Free Press.
Mock, W. B. T. (2011). Pareto optimality. In *Encyclopedia of global justice* (pp. 808–809). Springer.
Musgrave, R. A. (1959). *The theory of public finance*. McGraw Hill.
Neumann, I. B. (1999). *Uses of the Other: 'The East' in European identity formation*. University of Minnesota Press.
Olson, M. (1965). *The logic of collective action. Public goods and the theory of groups*. Harvard University Press.
Onuf, N. G. (1989). *A world of our making: rules and rule in social theory and international relations*. University of South Carolina Press.
Popa, F. (2015). Motivations to contribute to public goods: beyond rational choice economics. *Environmental Policy and Governance, 25*(4), 230–242.
Risse, T. (2000). Let's argue!': communicative action in world politics. *International Organization, 54*(1), 1–39.
Roberts, J. C. (2016). Constructing the Other: forming identities through ascribed preferences. *Towson University Journal of International Affairs, 49*(2), 43–58.
Roberts, J. C. (2019). *Constructing global public goods*. Lexington Books.
Samuelson, P. A. (1954). The pure theory of public expenditures. *Review of Economics and Statistics, 36*(4), 350–356.
Satz, D., & Ferejohn, J. (1994). Rational choice and social theory. *The Journal of Philosophy, 91*(2), 71–67.
Schumpeter, J. A. (1943). *Capitalism, socialism, and democracy*. George Allen & Unwin.
Simmel, G. (1950). The stranger. In K. H. Wolff (Ed.), *The sociology of Georg Simmel* (pp. 402–296). George Allen & Unwin.
Stigler, G. J., & Becker, G. S. (1977). De Gustibus Non Est Disputandum. *The American Economic Review, 67*(2), 76–90.
Von Neuman, J., & Morgenstern, O. (1944). *Theory of games and economic behaviour*. Princeton University Press.
Weinstein, E. A., & Deutchberger, P. (1963). Some dimensions of altercasting. *Sociometry, 26*(4), 454–466.
Wendt, A. (1987). The agent-structure problem in international relations theory. *International Organization, 41*(3), 335–370.
Wendt, A. (1992). Anarchy is what states make of It: the social construction of power politics. *International Organization, 46*(2), 391–425.
Wendt, A. (1994). Collective identity formation and the international state. *The American Political Science Review, 88*(2), 384–396.
Wendt, A. (1999). *Social theory of international politics*. Cambridge University Press.
Wichardt, P. C. (2008). Why and how identity should influence utility. University of Rostock-Department of Economics. Retrieved November 2022, from https://ssrn.com/abstract=878273

CHAPTER 4

'Unpacking' International Migration Governance: *Embeddedness* and Political Economy

INTRODUCTION

The multidisciplinary nature of migration is reflected in the huge amount of research in several social sciences branches, including economics (see Biffl, 2013), development (see Khondker, 2020), and demography (see Kritz, 2020). The history of the study of migration as an issue of politics in general and international relations in particular, has its origins in the 1990s. In this period, some historical events, such as the fall of the Berlin Wall in 1989 (followed by the end of the Soviet Union) or the signing of the Maastricht Treaty in 1992, forming the basis for the EU, were turning points and the beginning of the European integration process. In 1997, the Schengen Convention was incorporated into mainstream EU law by the Amsterdam Treaty. It came into effect in 1999, with the abolition of internal border controls in the EU, a milestone in the European integration project. Simultaneously, the Yugoslav wars compelled numerous refugees to seek asylum in European countries, triggering a significant crisis in migration management. In the late 1980s and in the 1990s, historical events like those mentioned above led researchers to study migration within the field of international relations through the security perspective. Despite some attempts at understanding migration dynamics through other international relations theories (see Hollifield, 1992), during the 1990s, the predominant branch of analysis was securitisation of migration (see Huysmans, 1995, 1997, 1998; Weiner, 1992). There has not been a consensus among scholars about which political sciences branch international migration should be categorised. Consequently, international migration has been perceived as a part of other political sciences fields rather than a unique area of enquiry.

In recent years, given the lack of an accepted theoretical framework for understanding international migration governance, some scholars have sought to explore more deeply the international relations dynamics behind global migration studies (see Betts & Loescher, 2011; Khalid, 2016). Although in past decades, there have been important advances in understanding the transnational dynamics behind international migration (see Castles & Alistair, 2000; Wimmer & Schille, 2002), the presence of multiple non-state political actors makes the study of international migration a difficult task. What has been extremely important has been consideration of the transnational nature of global migration governance.

In light of the novel nature of the issue, the increasing interest in the study of international migration has led the academic community to produce interesting literature about the political economy innate in international migration governance (see Betts, 2011; Newland, 2010). Scholars in the field have sought to put together the seeds of a theory of international migration from the political sciences, seeking to understand states' behaviour towards migration issues. This 'under-construction' theoretical framework—formed, in part, by the literature mentioned above—links the different types of migration with its governance. States construct in different ways different types of migration governance, depending on, (1) their interests/preferences, and (2) the type of migration in question. The lack of serious and coherent international migration governance (Betts, 2011) is reflected in the shortcomings in normative and institutional agreements at the global level. Over the past 20 years, in pursuit of a common theory of international migration, some scholars have initiated the seeds of a new heuristic framework based on the economic properties of the different types of migration (see Betts, 2011; Suhrke, 1998; Thielemann, 2018). This theoretical framework has become the standard framework to investigate refugee protection in international migration governance.

INTERNATIONAL MIGRATION GOVERNANCE

Structures from governance systems conform to informal institutions and actors that govern a specific issue field (Brumat et al., 2023). Governance processes refer to the interaction between the actors that compose governance institutions (Brumat et al., 2023). An obvious starting point is to outline the innate economic nature in migration governance. According to the Realist approach, states are perceived as actors that try to maximise their utilities to gain power (see Nicholson, 1998; Waltz, 1979; Wohlforth, 2007). Novel literature on international migration governance has focused on shedding light on states' behaviour towards migration phenomena, including the rationales behind states' formulation of migration policies.

When it comes to the form of joint inter-governmental production, international organisations are the main actors in providing global public goods. Nowadays, international organisations are central actors in international politics (Carbone, 2007). The provision of global public goods through international organisations (e.g., the UN, World Bank) reveal states' rationales—when the organisation provides a global public good, the members (states) may contribute to its provision so that their contribution is operationalised in the form of cooperation. At the international level, migration does not conform to governance itself as there is no strong global regulation framework. States act independently from international migration institutions, and the latters' regulations have little impact on states' actions in migration policymaking. The governance of migration is characterised by a fragmented basket of legislation and different regimes that regulate various types of human mobility (see Geddes, 2021). Certain types of migration governance are embedded in the international system of public goods characteristics (Betts, 2011; Chand & Markowski, 2018). Betts (2011) classifies migration governance into three types:

(a) Refugees → public good;
(b) Irregular and low-skilled migration → club good;
(c) High-skilled labour migration → private good.

In the first type, refugee governance is considered to have public benefits (non-excludable and non-rivalrous) for states. In the second, irregular and low-skilled migration is conceptualised as a club good with regional spillover and non-rivalrous and excludable benefits for states. Last but not least, high-skilled migration has excludable and rivalrous benefits for the states that admit these migrants to their territories. International organisations are important agents in promoting cooperation for reaching global goals and guaranteeing collective action success (Brumat et al., 2023).

They have a high degree of autonomy, set agendas, and promote regulations at the international level. When they are set up by states, they have a certain level of legitimacy to establish rules, backed by legislation, that promote the proper provision of global public goods. In the case of migration, they include the International Organization for Migration (IOM) and the United Nations High Commissioner for Refugees (UNCHR). The IOM and UNCHR are in charge of developing a solid system of international migration and asylum governance in cooperation with other political and non-political actors. The IOM manages the following areas of migration:[1] (1) migration and development; (2) facilitating migration; (3) regulating migration; (4) forced migration. The IOM is not regulated by international law, but despite this, in September 2016 it became a UN-affiliated international institution having some impact on other migrant organisations (Rossi, 2019). The IOM experiences a more independent role than the UNCHR, thus, the 'IOM never criticises its member-states and is unlikely to resist implementing projects that would be incompatible with its (non-existent) standards' (Rossi, 2019, p. 372). Contrary to the EU asylum and migration regime, characterised by a hierarchical structure, the international migration regime is not defined clearly and various actors (international organisations, states, stakeholders) manage migration with overlap in their decisions.

The degree of the UNCHR's authority and legitimacy has been claimed to be higher than the IOM (see Rossi, 2019). The UNCHR has sought to harmonise many aspects of the international migration system, especially in the field of forced migration. It cooperates with states by giving advice and supervising actions in crises involving displacement. With the lack of a consistent global migration system, states act on their own, provoking major political crises. In public goods terms, a governance system that is not well-integrated struggles to provide public goods (Caballero-Vélez & Pachocka, 2021). By the same token, non-integrated systems may correspond to problems in supplying global public goods. In the international arena, international organisations are important agents for promoting international cooperation and overcoming collective action problems (Brumat et al., 2023). The transnational nature of international migration has led scholars to find a common operationalisation of the regime, with no valuable results. Thus, due to its normative, humanitarian, sociological,

---

[1] Source: https://www.iom.int/about-iom.

and domestic characteristics, one may claim that there is no determined migration regime, rather there are several, depending on the approach taken.

INTERNATIONAL ASYLUM REGIME

Refugees are people whose home states do not provide fundamental rights, forcing them to seek refuge in another country. States' perceptions of migration differ depending on a few factors, such as history and identity, resulting in similar or different positions to the influx of refugees. The inherent cost-benefit factor in different types of migration governance from the individual (migrant) perspective has been studied by some scholars (Hollifield, 2007). Nevertheless, the cost-benefit calculus model from a state-centred perspective still remains un-researched due to the complexity of its empirical nature. Recent literature seeks to understand states' conditions on whether to accept refugees and to contribute to responsibility-sharing mechanisms in international asylum governance (e.g., Betts, 2003; Lutz & Portmann, 2022, Thielemann & Dewan, 2006). In the case of refugee protection, the mainstream assumption is that refugee protection provides collective benefits to states, while the costs are left to those states that admit refugees (Betts, 2003; Thielemann, 2003). Consequently, states tend to free-ride on other states' contributions to refugee protection, resulting in collective action failure. Refugees also provide, however, private benefits to host states, for instance, the economic benefits from forced migration have been discussed in welfare and migration literature (Betts, 2021). Increasing the economic benefits from refugees may lead to economic growth for individual states.

Refugee Protection as a Global Public Good

In her inspiring article, 'Burden-sharing during refugee emergencies: The logic of collective versus national action', Suhrke (1998) put roots on the theoretical model of refugee protection as a global public good. The underlying reasoning is that the provision of refugee protection provides public benefits to states (non-excludable and non-rivalrous). For instance, Suhrke identifies international stability and order as important benefits that accrue to all states regardless of their admission of refugees. The under-provision of refugee protection is the main consequence of the public nature of those benefits, as states tend to free-ride and avoid the admission of refugees to their territories.

Suhrke's foundational model has been groundbreaking for research in investigating public goods' characteristics in refugee protection. The foundational model's assumption lies on a static-Olsonian approach that assumes the public nature of benefits from refugee protection provision (Lutz & Caballero-Vélez, 2023). Betts (2003) calls into question this assumption by claiming the existence (also) of private benefits from refugee protection. Betts reflects on the private dimension of refugee protection by arguing that states' private incentives in admitting refugees may be to gain international prestige and to strengthen national security. The result of his investigation leads to an understanding of refugee protection as a 'joint product model' or 'impure public good'. Other scholars follow this assumption by expanding knowledge on the multi-dimensional nature (private and public) of refugee protection (Chand & Markowski, 2018; Roper & Barria, 2010). The free-riding problem raises the question of the degree of 'publicness' of refugee protection (Thielemann, 2018). Understanding the degree of 'publicness' of refugee protection may lead us to understand the different benefits of provision and states' commitment to responsibility-sharing mechanisms.

The provision of refugee protection provides numerous benefits to states and they vary in 'publicness' and 'globalness' (Lutz & Caballero-Vélez, 2023). In this regard, Lutz and Caballero-Vélez (2023) differentiate four types of benefits: legitimacy, security, development, and reputation. The first, fulfilling a moral and humanitarian legal obligation, is considered *legitimacy* benefits because significant refugee influxes undermine the liberal order (Lutz & Caballero-Vélez, 2023). Providing assistance to refugees is seen as a legitimacy repair mechanism (Bauböck, 2017), and restoring the damaged protection of human rights. Second, there are *security* benefits in the form of international stability and public order in other states (Betts, 2003). Nevertheless, some states may construct a perception of refugees as a threat; in that case, the perceived security benefits will be related to the national security and defence costs. Third, *development* benefits, refers to refugees' contributions to the host countries' economy and society (see D'Albis et al., 2018, Taylor et al., 2016). The fourth, *reputation* benefits, are the gain in international prestige from the state's protection of human rights.

States provide refugee protection when motivated by their own individual incentives and perception of benefits. States admit refugees depending on the perception of these benefits and how they overlap. For instance, a state motivated by recognition from the international community (prestige) will perceive refugee protection as a moral duty rather than a threat, and accordingly it will be motivated by the *reputation* and *legitimacy* incentives. On the other hand, states whose construct is refugees as a potential threat may perceive *legitimacy* benefits in a different way than states that seek to fulfil humanitarian legal norms. By understanding the construction of these benefits, we may see how states' maximisation of utility constitutes the public good. Next, I demonstrate how the rational-choice approach has limitations in the understanding of the responsibility-sharing dynamics by comparing the positivist utility model and the novel identity-utility model.

The Positivist Maximising Utility Model

Akerlof and Kranton's *Economics and Identity* (2000) refer to individuals' identities from an economic perspective, the individuals' utility in enhancing certain actions, and how involvement in a group or some social prescriptions may modify their utility in acting. If states are considered political actors by which governments are the subjects, actions enhanced by those governments will be the result of utility maximisation. Based on Akerlof and Kranton's (2000) model, in which V is utility, I_s the reduction of utility, and I_0 the loss of utility, refugee protection provision may be operationalised as follows:

- *Action 1*: accepting refugees; benefit = gain in utility (V)
- *Action 2*: accepting some refugees; benefits and costs = reduction of utility ($V - I_s$)
- *Action 3*: not accepting any refugees; cost = loss of utility ($V - I_0$)

If utility is about maximising benefits, then: $V = V(b_1 + b_2 + ...+ b_3)$. This utility ($V$) would be considered as pertaining to the individual's action. By enhancing action 1, there is an increase in utility, and action 2 means a loss of utility or it is the same as the sum of the costs:

- *Action 1:* $V(b_1 + b_2 + ... + b_3)$
- *Action 3*: $V - I_0 (c_1 + c_2 + ... + c_3)$

Accordingly, the calculation of a state's utility is as follows:

$$u^i = V(b_1 + b_2 + \ldots + b_3) > V - I_0(c_1 + c_2 + \ldots + c_3)$$

The state's final individual utility is determined when the utility of accepting refugees (action 1) is higher than not accepting refugees (action 3). If we take the maximising benefits model by Popa (2015) as our calculation, it is indexed as follows:

$$u^i = X^i(B^x) > Y^i(B^Y)$$

In this formula, we see how the state (i) increases its utility (u) as it increases the benefits perceived from providing refugee protection (X) versus the benefits of not providing refugee protection (Y). By providing refugee protection (X), states may gain net benefits in the form of development, security, prestige, and legitimacy (B^x); on the other hand, non-provision of refugee protection (Y) conceives a net benefit in national security and/or defence (B^Y). Within the framework of this criterion, a state's utility (u^i) would increase if the state perceives that the net benefit of providing refugee protection is higher than the net benefit of not admitting refugees.

For instance, in a calculation in which the benefit is international recognition by other states, the cost is a security threat, and the state decides to provide refugee protection because the perception of international recognition and fulfilling humanitarian legal norms is higher that the perception of refugees as a security threat to its territory, a formula that might represent the situation is as follows:

$$X_n = X^i((B^x) > (C^x))$$

The provision of refugee protection (X_n) is determined by the perception of the public good by the state (X^i) as a higher preference of international prestige and recognition by providing refugee protection (B^x) than the cost of perceiving refugees as a security threat (C^x). Whether or not this model provides empirical validation of the maximising-behaviour rationale behind states' refugee protection provision, it lacks an explanation of the motivations behind the states' perception of refugee protection as a benefit (international prestige) rather than a cost (security threat).

The Identity Utility-Model

This research makes an in-depth analysis of the formulation of preferences towards the net benefit and net costs by claiming that a state's norms, customs, and identity,[2] influence its utility and preferences towards refugee protection. Diagram 4.1 shows how a state's identity (formed by customs and norms) influences its perception of the benefits and utility increase of an action. By the same token, identity determines a state's own perception of reality. The first stage of the provision process is when state A has a binary choice: accepting refugees or not. In the first case, the state's identity maximises the utility of accepting refugees, perceived as a benefit. In a context in which refugee protection is regularised, this would be the appropriate decision because the social dimension is positive. The first source of the state's choice of accepting refugees is its own identity, which shapes its preferences according to a 'logic of appropriateness'. The final stage refers to the production of the public good (refugee protection).

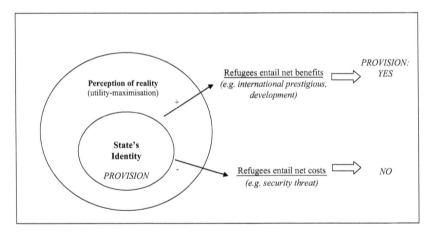

Diagram 4.1 A state's construction of preferences. (Source: Own elaboration)

[2] International Relations (IR) scholars have identified a state's identity in a collective action scenario as the main source of the state's formation of preferences (See Wendt, 1992). Though this paper is based on the latest assumptions, in order to instrumentalise state's choices, I refer to a state's identity as that viewed by the government in power (unit of enquiry).

In a collective action scenario, state A may perceive refugee protection as having more benefits than costs, while state B does not; in Wendt's words (1994): 'The ability to overcome collective action problems depends in part on whether actors' social identities generate self-interests or collective interests (...) sometimes defined so as to subsume altruism, which makes explanations of behaviour in such terms tautological' (p. 386).

From Wendt's assumption, one may realise that these collective interests may be reflected in the creation of policy regimes in order to regulate a certain issue. In the case of migration, the development of an international migration regime might be seen as the goal of the collective interests of states. Having described earlier how weak the international migration regime is, it is clear that there is a predominance of national interests rather than collective interests. In security terms, depending on the externalities and geographical levels of effect, a state may perceive refugees as a threat and not assist them. The perceived individual (private) security incentives may lead a state to reinforce border control and/or take other actions to increase its national security policies.

THE EU MIGRATION REGIME

Due to the complexity of the EU foundations and legal system (there are three main types of competences: EU exclusive competences, shared competences with Member States, EU supporting competences), and therefore also of governance in various policy fields, analysis of the production of public goods may be conducted by looking at a specific policy domain where shared competences are applied. When Member States are interested in contributing to the provision of a public good (normally by transferring competences to the organisation), the EU sets up tools such as legal norms, shared unwritten values, and good practices to provide regional public goods with spillover to all Member States.

The EU migration and asylum regime is difficult to define in terms of regulation.[3] There is not just one policy concerning EU migration and asylum issues, but many:

---

[3] Balch and Geddes (2011) use 'regime' instead of 'policy' in reference to the complex systems of legal forms that, on an EU basis, regulate the organisation's migration and asylum policies.

(1) *Integration-immigration policy*: corresponds to all EU legal and political documents pertaining to the integration process of third-country nationals in the EU; third-country nationals have rights and obligations in relation to the host country and other EU Member States (Gońda et al., 2020). Integration is not considered a separate policy and has an interdependency relationship with immigration policy (Gońda et al., 2020). For a well-functioning immigration policy, integration must work properly.
(2) *Asylum policy*: refers both to EU legal acts and political decisions regarding offering international protection to third-country nationals seeking it (based on the *principle of non-refoulement*).

In recent years, EU enlargement has tabled some key questions about the willingness of new Member States to cooperate on these issues (Balch & Geddes, 2011). In particular, issues such as border security, asylum, and irregular migration have raised some questions about the type of cooperation in the EU (Thielemann & Armstrong, 2013). Considering the layers of the EU migration and asylum regime, some scholars have identified the economic dynamics behind some migration and asylum policy areas. In the case of asylum policy, Thielemann and Amstrong (2013) analysed the public goods characteristics of the Dublin Regulation.[4] Betts (2003) underlines some important costs and benefits mechanisms behind EU burden-sharing mechanisms. Thielemann (2018) explored the dynamics of public goods behind refugee protection provision. One may argue that not all migration and asylum policies follow the same costs/benefits calculus, as Member States perceive different types of migration in the EU in different ways. Intra-EU migration of those enjoying the freedom of movement from one Member State to another (for work or study) may bring benefits for the host country. At the same time, it may also produce benefits for the sending country, for example, students' mobility under the Erasmus+ student exchange programme. For migrants from third countries, the situation may be different, with the Member States having different positions towards it, so the EU act not with just one voice but many.

[4] 'The Dublin Regulation identifies the Member State as responsible for the examination of the asylum application. The criteria for establishing responsibility run, in hierarchical order, from family considerations, to recent possession of a visa or residence permit in a Member State, to whether the applicant has entered the EU irregularly, or regularly' (Source: https://ec.europa.eu/home-affairs/what-we-do/policies/asylum/examination-of-applicants_en) (date: 18-11-2022).

The Regulation of Refugee Protection as a European Public Good

The provision of refugee protection in EU law is regulated by the treaties and the Charter of Fundamental Rights (EU primary law) and directives and regulations (EU secondary law), among others. EU asylum policy is settled by legal measures and the tools within the Common European Asylum System (CEAS). The EU attempts to build up the common framework for international refugee protection as the Member States seek to contribute legally, institutionally, and politically to setting up common regional standards in the field of refugee protection (Caballero-Vélez & Pachocka, 2021). EU asylum law, and specifically the development of a common CEAS, is based on the 1951 Geneva Convention on the protection of refugees, the first international legal measure recognising international protection as a fundamental right.

The multilevel governance nature, with roles for numerous political and non-political actors, makes the CEAS a very complex legal system in the EU asylum regime. In order to clarify its operationalisation, I will examine CEAS policymaking by using Langford's pyramid model (2013) to explain the different dependencies of this kind of policy system (Fig. 4.1):

At the base of the pyramid, the Geneva Convention is the 'foundation' from which the EU asylum regime is built. In the case of refugee protection, it puts international protection at a human right level, thus prohibiting the refoulement of asylum-seekers to territories where they risk death or torture (Langford, 2013). In the middle of the pyramid, primary EU law (treaties) builds on the Geneva Convention to further develop the CEAS. To complement the treaties, EU secondary law—in this group we may find directives, regulations, and so on—caps the highest level of this theoretical pyramid. In order to build a consolidated CEAS, all parts of the pyramid must be fulfilled by the Member States. In the case of secondary EU law, Member States are sometimes reluctant towards cooperation on some asylum issues and the implementation of EU law into their national legislations; among them are:

(1) *EU primary law*: the EU Charter of Fundamental Rights, specifically, its Art. 19,[5] Right to Asylum; and the Treaties, in particular

---

[5] Art. 19 of the EU Charter of Fundamental Rights: 'The right to asylum shall be guaranteed with due respect for the rules of the Geneva Convention of 28 July 1951 and the Protocol of 31 January 1967 relating to the status of refugees and in accordance with the Treaty on European Union and the Treaty on the Functioning of the European Union'.

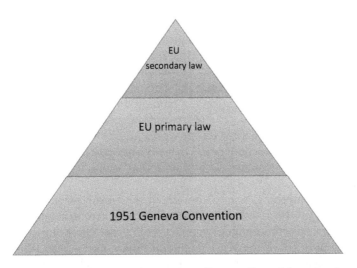

Fig. 4.1 Pyramid of the EU asylum regime. (Source: Own elaboration, based on Langford (2013))

Art. 78(1) of the TFUE.[6] As mentioned above, the principle of non-refoulement is emphasised, confirming that the EU regional refugee protection regime has its roots in international refugee law (Caballero-Vélez & Pachocka, 2021). At this level, some institutions such as the European Court of Human Rights and the Court of Justice of the EU play roles in asylum issues.

(2) *EU secondary law*: The treaties and Charter legislation provide the standards to develop the common legal framework through EU secondary law (i.e., directives and regulations). In this regard, EU asylum policy is operationalised, forming the Common European Asylum System (Caballero-Vélez & Pachocka, 2021). At this level, we may situate the Dublin Regulation.

---

[6] Art. 78(1) of the TFUE: 'The Union shall develop a common policy on asylum, subsidiary protection and temporary protection with a view to offering appropriate status to any third-country national requiring international protection and ensuring compliance with the principle of non-refoulement. This policy must be in accordance with the Geneva Convention of 28 July 1951 and the Protocol of 31 January 1967 relating to the status of refugees, and other relevant treaties'.

While refugee protection is provided by EU law, serious doubts have been raised about the efficacy of its provision through the Member States. In recent years, and in particular due to the massive influx of refugees in 2015, there has been a visible lack of solidarity between the Member States in providing international protection. Though international protection to those fleeing war or persecution is a binding duty on the Member States, many competences related to asylum and migration issues remain at the national level. Consequently, this provokes numerous legal complications emanating from EU secondary law that were not correctly implemented at the national level, resulting in a regime that seems to be always under construction.

Refugee protection may be considered the 'cornerstone' of the EU's asylum policy—the so-called refugee or international protection policy—which together with immigration policy and border checks form the three basic components of the EU's migration policy, part of the EU area of freedom, security, and justice (Caballero-Vélez & Pachocka, 2021). This policy area is characterised by the 'shared' nature of competences between the EU and Member States; in other words, the European Union and the Member States may regulate such policy based on Art. 67 (1)(2) of the TFUE,[7] which reads:

(1) The Union shall constitute an area of freedom, security, and justice with respect for fundamental rights and the different legal systems and traditions of the Member States.
(2) It shall ensure the absence of internal border controls for persons and shall frame a common policy on asylum, immigration, and external border control, based on solidarity between Member States, which is fair towards third-country nationals. For the purpose of this Title, stateless persons shall be treated as third-country nationals'.

Thus, refugee protection is considered a European public good that is provided by the EU efficiently. It may be considered European because it is provided by the EU, and it is public because it provides non-rivalrous and non-excludable benefits. In order for refugee protection to become a European public good, though, national governments must implement in their national law all regulations needed to provide effective protection at

[7] Treaty on the Functioning of the European Union.

the EU level. As solidarity (unanimity in voting) is one of the bases of migration and asylum policy, in many cases, the Member States are not obligated to implement such regulations in their national legislation. This situation leads to ineffective provision of refugee protection by EU institutions. In this case, the Member States' perceptions of the benefits and costs of refugee protection differ from each other, provoking a situation of collective action failure and the subsequent effect of a poorly integrated policy area.

During crises, those Member States that do not have a fully developed national asylum regime are unable to contribute to the development of a common CEAS. If not all of the Member States have the same interests in relation to asylum, their perceptions of international protection to refugees will differ from each other. Refugee protection emanates both benefits and costs for Member States, so under-provision of it is the result of a weak CEAS system, as well as the reliance on not solid national asylum systems. In EU terms, the under-provision of refugee protection is provoked by the lack of integration in EU asylum and migration policy.

Conclusions

Different types of migration governance have public goods characteristics. Understanding the social and institutional dimensions of a state's actions is an important factor in deciphering states' preferences in formulation migration policies. The rational choice approach (logic of consequences-maximising-benefits rationale) has strong limitations in explaining states' motivations in making different choices. A state's decision to allow refugees onto its territory or not depends on how its self-identity is shaped by behaviour norms and perceived utility.

When it comes to the asylum regime, the EU may be considered part of the social dimension of action by which Member States (actors/agents) act according to EU norms/rules. Nevertheless, when a crisis arises, the Member States may follow their own interests, which may be the opposite of the EU institutions. The effect of agents' own logic of action in opposition to the social dimension logic of 'appropriateness' has not been examined in detail, and normally it has been argued that the social dimension shapes states' interests. The Member States might perceive refugees as a threat, which modifies their national interests and willingness to embrace collective action. Accordingly, EU migration policies have a two-level kind of governance; in other words, they are made in cooperation with the

Member States, whose interests and environment play a crucial role in their policymaking process unless there is a 'critical juncture' (crisis) in which those policies can change. In EU terms, strong integration is therefore understood as the substitution of separate national regimes with common EU policies and a commitment from the Member States to narrowly implement the content of EU legislation.

A number of tentative conclusions about the study of Member State actions through the logic-of-consequences approach may be that, in the context of a migration crisis, Member States seek to maximise their utility in providing international protection or not. Nevertheless, this approach's main shortcoming relies on the point that the social dimension does not influence the Member States' decisions at all. In this case, the EU (norms, institutions, and rules) might be placed in this analysis as the social dimension in which the Member States interact, so, consequently, from a logical perspective under this approach, the Member States choose to act with respect to a migration crisis by following their own interests and not taking into consideration EU norms.

REFERENCES

Akerlof, G. A., & Kranton, R. E. (2000). Economics and identity. *The Quarterly Journal of Economics, 115*(3), 715–753.
Balch, A., & Geddes, A. (2011). The development of the EU migration and asylum regime. In H. Dijstelbloem & A. Meijer (Eds.), *Migration and the new technological borders of Europe* (pp. 22–39). Palgrave Macmillan.
Bauböck, R. (2017). Refugee protection and burden-sharing in the European Union. *Journal of Common Market Studies, 56*(1), 141–156.
Betts, A. (2003). 'Public goods theory and the provision of refugee protection: The role of the joint-product model in burden-sharing theory. *Journal of Refugee Studies, 16*(3), 274–296.
Betts, A. (2011). *Global migration governance*. Oxford University Press.
Betts, A. (2021). *The wealth of refugees: How displaced people can build economies*. Oxford University Press.
Betts, A., & Loescher, G. (2011). *Refugees in international relations*. Oxford University Press.
Biffl, G. (2013). The role of migration in economic relations between Europe and Turkey. *European Review, 21*, 372–381.
Brumat, L., Caballero-Vélez, D., & Pachocka, M. (2023). The role of international organizations in global migration governance: Sustainable development as a strategy for extending global public goods. In E. Latoszek, & A. Kłos

(eds.), *Global public goods and sustainable development in the practice of international organizations. responding to challenges of today's world*. Brill.
Caballero-Vélez, D., & Pachocka, M. (2021). Producing public goods in the EU: European integration processes in the fields of refugee protection and climate stability. *European Politics and Society, 22*(1), 1–18.
Carbone, M. (2007). Supporting or resisting global public goods. *Global Governance, 13*(2), 179–198.
Castles, S., & Alistair, D. (2000). *Citizenship and migration: Globalization and the politics of belonging*. Routledge.
Chand, S., & Markowski, S. (2018). ANZ-Pacific migration governance system. *International Migration, 57*(5), 294–308.
Charter of Fundamental Rights of the European Union. (2010). *Official Journal of the European Union* C83, vol. 53, European Union.
D'Albis, H., Boubtane, E., & Coulibaly, D. (2018). Macroeconomic evidence suggests that asylum seekers are not a 'burden' for Western European countries, *Science. Advances, 4*(6), eaaq0883.
Geddes, A. (2021). *Governing migration beyond the state: Europe, North America, South America, and Southeast Asia in a global context*. Oxford University Press.
Gońda, M., Lesińska, M., & Pachocka, M. (2020). Relations between immigration and integration policies in postwar Europe. In M. Duszczyk, M. Pachocka, & D. Pszczółkowska (Eds.), *Relations between immigration and integration policies in Europe* (pp. 24–45). Routledge.
Hollifield, J. F. (1992). *Immigrants, markets and states*. Harvard University Press.
Hollifield, J. F. (2007). The politics of immigration and the rise of the migration state. In R. Ueda (Ed.), *A companion to American immigration* (pp. 132–158). Blackwell.
Huysmans, J. (1995). Migrants as a security problem: Dangers of 'securitizing' societal issues. In R. Miles & D. Thränhardt (Eds.), *Migration and European integration: The dynamics of inclusion and exclusion* (pp. 53–72). Fairleigh Dickinson University Press, Pinter Publishers.
Huysmans, J. (1997). Security—technique or techniques? A discussion of the complexity of the meaning of security. Paper for Journée d'étude: Risque, menaces et peurs de l'immigration—sentiments d'insécurité et processus de sécurité, CERI, Paris.
Huysmans, J. (1998). Security! What do you mean? From concept to thick signifier. *European Journal of International Relations, 4*(2), 226–255.
Khalid, K. (2016). *International migration: A very short introduction* (2nd ed.). Oxford University Press.
Khondker, H. H. (2020). Development Studies and Migration. In C. Inglis, W. Li, & B. Khadria (Eds.), *The Sage handbook of international migration* (pp. 42–53). SAGE Publications Ltd.

Kritz, M. M. (2020). Demography. In C. Inglis, W. Li, & B. Khadria (Eds.), *The Sage handbook of international migration* (pp. 42–53). SAGE Publications Ltd.

Langford, L. M. (2013). The other Euro crisis: Rights violations under the Common European Asylum System and the unraveling of EU solidarity. *Harvard Human Rights Journal, 26*, 217–264.

Lutz, P., & Caballero-Vélez, D. (2023). The public nature of refugee protection: What benefits for states?' Paper presented at the Migration Policy Centre, Schuman Centre of Advanced Studies (European University Institute), Florence, IT.

Lutz, P., & Portmann, L. (2022). Why do states admit refugees? A comparative analysis of resettlement policies in OECD countries. *Journal of Ethnic and Migration Studies, 48*(11), 2515–2539.

Newland, K. (2010). The governance of international migration: Mechanisms, processes and institutions. *Global Governance, 16*(3), 331–344.

Nicholson, M. (1998). Realism and utopianism revisited. *Review of International Studies, The Eighty Years' Crisis, 1919–1999(24)*, 65–82.

Popa, F. (2015). Motivations to contribute to public goods: Beyond rational choice economics. *Environmental Policy and Governance, 25*(4), 230–242.

Roper, S. D., & Barria, L. A. (2010). 'Burden sharing in the funding of the UNHCR: Refugee protection as an impure public good. *Journal of Conflict Resolution, 54*(4), 616–637.

Rossi, R. (2019). The role of the International Organization for Migration and the UNHCR in the EU and Italy: Still entrapped by a securitization approach to Mediterranean migration? *Contemporary Italian Politics, 11*(4), 369–385.

Suhrke, A. (1998). Burden-sharing during refugee emergencies: The logic of collective versus national action. *Journal of Refugee Studies, 11*(4), 396–415.

Taylor, J. Edward, Mateusz J. Filipski, Mohamad Alloush, and Ernesto González-Estrada. (2016). Economic Impact of Refugees. *Proceedings of the National Academy of Sciences, 113*(27), 7449–7453.

Thielemann, E. (2003). Between interests and norms: Explaining burden-sharing in the European Union. *Journal of Refugee Studies, 16*(3), 253–273.

Thielemann, E. (2018). Why refugee burden-sharing initiatives fail: Public goods, free- riding and symbolic solidarity in the EU. *Journal of Common Market Studies, 56*(1), 63–82.

Thielemann, E., & Armstrong, C. (2013). Understanding European asylum cooperation under the Schengen/Dublin system: A public goods framework. *European Security, 22*(2), 148–164.

Thielemann, E., & Dewan, T. (2006). The myth of free-riding: Refugee protection and implicit burden-sharing. *West European Politics, 29*(2), 351–369.

Treaty on European Union and the Treaty on the Functioning of the European Union [2016] OJ C202/1 (TFEU).

Waltz, K. N. (1979). *Theory of international politics*. Random House.

Weiner, M. (1992). Security, stability and international migration. *International Security*, *17*(3), 91–126.

Wendt, A. (1992). Anarchy is what states make of it: The social construction of world politics. *International Organization*, *46*(2), 391–425.

Wendt, A. (1994). Collective identity formation and the international state. *The American Political Science Review*, *88*(2), 384–396.

Wimmer, A., & Schille, N. G. (2002). Methodological nationalism and beyond: Nation-state building, migration and the social sciences. *Global Networks*, *2*(4), 301–334.

Wohlforth, W. C. (2007). Realism and foreign policy. In A. Smith, A. Hadfield, & T. Dunne (Eds.), *Foreign policy: Theories, actors, cases* (pp. 31–48). Oxford University Press.

CHAPTER 5

Security or Humanitarianism? The Paradigm of Refugee Protection on Central-Eastern European Borders

INTRODUCTION

Since the mid-1990s, the EU has sought to combine both the processes of opening intra-European borders and closing external borders. The security-related motivations behind this 'closing door' policy is, in part, due to the European enlargement process that has brought the union closer to less-democratic neighbours and the experience of terrorism, irregular migration flows, and Russian aggression (Eilstrup-Sangiovanni, 2021). The initial main concern of the Eastern enlargement project was the differences between the Western European economies and those of the candidate states. The Yugoslavia crisis led the EU to increasingly be wary of other non- economic issues that could encompass the membership of these countries to the Union, including issues more related to Justice and Home Affairs (JHA), such as security (Phuong, 2003). It was a major step for the security agenda to integrate these countries into the European project, so the important issue was to understand the capacity of Central-Eastern European governments in strengthening border-control management (Phuong, 2003), especially in cases of massive influxes of migrants. In this context, solidarity becomes a fundamental key for managing migration flows in the EU (Milazzo, 2023).

According to Thym and Tsourdi (2017), the concept of solidarity has several facets, including moral, social, political, and legal considerations.

© The Author(s), under exclusive license to Springer Nature Switzerland AG 2023
D. Caballero-Vélez, *Contesting Migration Crises in Central Eastern Europe*, Mobility & Politics,
https://doi.org/10.1007/978-3-031-44037-3_5

While there are no barriers to defining solidarity's moral component within the framework of EU immigration and refugee legislation, its legal nature is still up for debate. There is no definition in the Treaty, despite the fact that the ideas of solidarity and equitable responsibility are incorporated in Article 80 TFEU. However, it is important to remember that the Member States do have legal obligations that cannot and should not be readily discarded: first and principally, due to the fact that a hard law provision incorporates the solidarity principle. Inter-state solidarity calls for Member States 'shall assist each other in carrying out tasks which flow from the Treaties', particularly in the areas of asylum, migration, and border controls (Goldner Lang, 2022). This is in accordance with the responsibility of sincere cooperation.

On 23 September 2020, the European Commission launched the New Pact on Migration, whose purpose was to reform Dublin IV by 'forming the basis of a reliable common migration and asylum system'. One of the major parts of the New Pact on Migration (NPM) manoeuvres around the concepts of 'solidarity' and 'responsibility', and in this regard, the Pact introduced the idea of 'flexible solidarity' by which the Member States should contribute in supporting first-entry states facing a massive influx of arrivals. The Commission sought to put some distance to binding measures, proposing instead individual substantial contributions. Among these measures, we see the acceptance of relocating asylum-seekers and taking on the responsibility of the return of migrants with no right to stay. On this subject, the adoption of flexible measures may be seen as an attempt to share the costs of refugee protection. In public goods terms, scholarship has provided insights on the mixed benefits that arise from collective actions (Sandler, 1977; Sandler & Forbes, 1980). With the high political contestation in EU frontline states, different outcomes will depend on cost-benefits negotiations (Schimmelfennig, 2021). In the context of Central Eastern European (CEE) borders, frontline Member States will employ either an open- or closed-door policy based on their perception of utility maximisation in providing refugee protection. The Pact is thus a legal act aimed at finding compromise between mandatory solidarity, sought by Southern Member States, and the 'flexible solidarity' demanded by Visegrad countries.

This chapter provides information gathered from interviews conducted with experts on migration in Poland. These interviews were conducted in 2020, so before the Russian invasion of Ukraine in early 2022. They show how before the 2021 and 2022 migration crises on the EU's eastern border, the Polish government was already pursuing a dual approach towards migrants from Eastern Europe and the Middle East. The timing of these interviews is crucial to understanding how Poland has dealt with the recent crises.

The 2021 Poland-Belarus Border Crisis: A Security Response

Between July and December 2021, there was a migration crisis at Lithuania's, Latvia's, and Poland's eastern borders. Belarusian President Alexander Lukashenko's declaration to open borders and allow up to 50,000 migrants to enter Poland marked the escalation of a political crisis. Even if West-East political ties were somewhat normalised at the time, these kinds of occurrences caused political tensions between the two blocs in Europe to increase. With the establishment of the European Agency for the Management of Operational Cooperation at the External Borders (FRONTEX, now the European Border and Coast Guard Agency) and efforts to secure its eastern borders in 2004, the EU made concrete efforts to secure its external borders.

In 2021, migrants seeking to enter the EU were mainly from Kurdish Iraq, Syria, and Yemen, with Belarus encouraging and, in some cases, forcing them to cross the Eastern EU border. In August, Belarus funded flights from Sulaymaniyah, Erbil, and Basra in Iraq to Minsk, and Lithuanian intelligence found that Belarusian authorities were promoting cheap vacations and visas to the EU. The response of the border countries affected by the crisis was to mobilise their border guards and military to the borders: a kind of no-man's land was created, where the Latvian and Polish armies stopped the migrants at the border, while the Belarusian border guards and the Belarusian army stood on the other side and behind the migrants to stop them in a narrow strip of mostly forested border territory. The Polish government stepped up its 'closed door' policy, with Polish border guards conducting 'pushbacks' (physically pushing people back across the border). At the same time, Warsaw refused to accept applications for international protection. Humanitarian activist groups, including NGOs and researchers, provided most of the support for the refugees. Because Poland imposed a state of emergency in the border region (which restricted access to the public and public information), it was difficult to compile reliable daily information about what was happening at the border. A law allowing rapid deportation and permission for the construction of a continuous border fence were granted. The humanitarian crisis on the Belarusian-Polish border has shown that the migration issue has become a matter of foreign policy action rather than an internal EU conflict. The Polish response was led by Prime Minister Morawiecki, who decried Belarus' attempts to 'destabilise' Europe and called on the Member States to stand together to defend Europe. Law and Justice politicians (and other right-wing parties) saw political opportunity in posing this threat to Poland's national territory and sought to use the crisis as a uniting feature in a mutual stand against threats from Belarus and Russia. These events led this migration influx to be considered as a 'hybrid threat', reinforcing the idea of 'Fortress Europe'. This concept alludes to the increasing securitisation of migration and its control at European borders. It also refers to how border control has become a fundamental part of EU asylum policies as a result of the externalisation of this issue. In addition, the Poland-Belarus border crisis led Brussels to use the notion of 'Fortress Europe' in security and defence policies (External Action Area of the Union) in reference to threats outside the EU's borders and the need to strengthen cooperation in defence and security matters, especially some aspects that are gaining prominence. One of those is encapsulated in a new but rare term, 'crimmigration', or the criminalisation of migration. Although this concept is part of the terminology of the criminological study of border control, the narrative construction of the migrant as a criminal has been used by populist movements to refer to a Europe in which strong and rigid border control is necessary to prevent threats such as terrorism or organised crime.

In the 2015 refugee crisis, Poland strictly opposed the potential allocation of some of the refugees in the EU who had come from Middle East countries. This contrasted with its policy towards Eastern European migrants. It justified it like this: 'when it comes to migrants from Ukraine and Eastern countries, it's definitely possible to integrate them in our society, but when it comes to those who came from Middle East countries the situation is bit different, the integration process is harder and the difficult is due to the language, due to the culture, due to completely different origin roots and cultural differences' (EX7, interview October 2020). In interviews, respondents commonly stated that Middle East migrants are perceived by the Polish government as a security threat. As mentioned above, this was reflected by the change of government in 2014 and, consequently, the position of the Polish government to the 2016 Refugee

Relocation Scheme. In this case, interview EX3 notes the change, that while the Civic Platform (Platforma Obwatelska, PO) government agreed to take part in the programme, when the Prawo i Sprawiedliwość (Law and Justice party)-led government coalition took power, they blocked it; in one official's words, they said: 'no, we don't want to welcome any refugees from Syria, Lebanon or other countries, especially from Libya and Syria' (EX3 interview, October 2020). Broadly speaking, even if some refugees/asylum-seekers from these countries were highly skilled migrants, Law and Justice politicians do not perceive them as an economic resource for Poland, only as a potential threat.

The 2022 Ukrainian Refugee Crisis: A Humanitarian Response

The 2022 Russian invasion of Ukraine provoked a major influx of refugees from that country to the EU, at first, mostly to Poland. The EU responded to the invasion with a package of sanctions against Russia and Belarus (economic, financial, diplomatic, and political). The European Union implemented the 2021 Temporary Protection Directive (TPD) for the first time in response to a refugee crisis.[1] The TPD was adopted in 2001 to cope with the people fleeing the Yugoslav war and provoked the EU to re-formulate the European asylum system that was, at that moment, incapable of dealing with such a large forced-displacement challenge. The rationale behind the TPD was merely to avoid situations in which the Member States did not have common positions on the rights granted to migrants—in other words, it constituted a burden-sharing mechanism. On 2 March 2022, the Commission proposed to activate the TPD, and the European Council supported this imitative through a Decision confirming the existence of a situation of a mass influx of migrants.[2] The Directive itself had a completely different nature than the Dublin System as it sought to overcome the lack of cooperation among the Member States to alleviating frontline Member States through the allocation of migrants (so-called quotas). Contrary to the Poland-Belarus border crisis

---

[1] European Council, «Directive 2001/55/EC of 20 July 2001 on minimum standards for giving temporary protection in the event of a mass influx of displaced persons and on measures promoting a balance of efforts between Member States in receiving such persons and bearing the consequences thereof», OJ L 212, 7 August 2001, p. 12–23.

[2] Council Implementing Decision (EU) 2022/382 of 4 March 2022.

the year earlier, in which that migration flow was framed as a 'hybrid threat' to the EU, there was now strong support for the Member States to collaborate on the allocation of Ukrainian refugees. Apart from the TDP, the EU launched an internet platform for people fleeing Ukraine that contained all the necessary information for expediting their entry. All these measures, along with financial support to the host countries, supposed a spirit of strong support of and solidarity with Ukraine, leading even to an acceleration of the discussion of prospective future Ukrainian membership in the EU.

Poland enhanced its open-door policy for Ukrainian migrants, becoming the primary first destination country for people fleeing Ukraine. The response was multi-level, with a key role for NGOs and local governments, particularly border towns such as Przemysl and big cities such as Warsaw, Cracow, Lublin, Wroclaw, and Gdansk. In addition, the huge support from volunteers, private persons, to the Ukrainian diaspora ('social solidarity') led to a major humanitarian response. The Polish government passed the 2022 Law on assistance to Ukrainian citizens, a legal and institutional framework to support Ukrainian citizens in the context of the war. This contrasted with the response in 2014, when Russia occupied Crimea and there was a small increase of Ukrainian migrants fleeing to Poland (EX5, interview October 2020)—most of them were accepted as migrant workers rather than asylum seekers (EX1, interview September 2020). Before the 2022 Ukrainian forced migration flows, most of the Ukrainians in Poland were considered economic or education-seeking migrants, and in the case of those fleeing Crimea earlier, these migrants decided to apply for work permission instead of asylum (EX2, interview September 2020).

During the interviews, the respondents commonly agreed with the view that Eastern European migrants, even those unofficially refugees (people who fled conflict zones but did not have refugee protection) are perceived by the Polish government as an economic resource for the country. Regarding this group of migrants, in the case of Ukrainians (the major group of Eastern European migrants in Poland), they are perceived as people similar to Poles, as EX5 noted: 'we have a similar language, similar history, that at one point was quite problematic, the relation between Poland and Ukraine, but in general we have the same heritage, European heritage, but it is like Central-Eastern European heritage, so I think it should be easier for them to accommodate here in Poland' (interview October 2020).

Even before the 2022 Russian full-scale invasion of Ukraine, one could expect that in a situation of a massive influx of Eastern European migrants arriving in Poland, the government would have an open-door approach towards them, as EX3 stated: 'we accept more than one million economic migrants from Ukraine, but do not accept any refugees from the Middle East' (interview, September 2020). The unstable political situation in Belarus before the invasion had already led the Polish government to be prepared for a situation in which a mass of Belarusian refugees would come to Poland; as EX7 stated, 'Poland would have opened the borders to them, not only because many Poles live there but also the identification with similar cultural values and similar traditions' (interview, October 2020).

CONCLUSIONS

This chapter has emphasised Poland's different approach towards Middle Eastern migrants and Eastern European migrants, especially Ukrainians. These seemingly similar situations have been handled in different ways, and, most importantly, the interviews—conducted before the Russian full-scale invasion—even predicted the Polish government's open-door policy to Ukrainians. The security-humanitarian approach is the line that has been predominant in the EU. European governments may change their positions towards a migration crisis, alternatively demanding 'solidarity' or a lack of cooperation. The case of Poland is worthy of study, given the two different responses to similar situations, reflecting the cost-benefit rationales behind the Polish government's migration policymaking, even though the categorisation of migrants (refugees, economic migrants, asylum-seekers) is politically constructed to support their actions. In the case of Poland, before the war, most Ukrainians accepted into the country were economic migrants, but the narrative relayed to Brussels was that they were refugees. By the same token, in 2022, Poland continued its friendly approach towards Ukrainians by granting them with international protection. Completely different actions were visible in the case of Middle Eastern migrants. In the 2015 and 2016 refugee crises, there was a clear lack of solidarity by Central-Eastern European governments to relocating refugees, and in the 2022 border crisis, Poland halted refugees and carried out pushbacks along the Polish-Belarusian border.

EU refugee governance marked by a security-humanitarian dichotomy of Member States' national sovereignty and fulfilling European and international humanitarian law form what seems like a constant dilemma for the functioning of the EU asylum system. As the European Union attempts to find a solution to this, it has settled for now on a 'flexible solidarity' approach towards forced-displacement situations. The Member States' humanitarian-security dynamics may be analysed through a cost-benefit calculus model. In this regard, 'flexible solidarity' may be seen as an attempt to find the equilibrium in the humanitarian-security dilemma. The different policies enacted towards similar forced-displacement situations are the result of the differences in the states' formation of the costs and benefits. Governments enhance their migration policies depending on their perceptions of the states' norms, customs, and identities. In Chap. 6, I show how Poland's norms and customs may be determinant in the formation of preferences towards refugees.

References

Council Implementing Decision (EU) 2022/382 of 4 March 2022.
Eilstrup-Sangiovanni, M. (2021). Re-bordering Europe? Collective action barriers to 'Fortress Europe. *Journal of European Public Policy, 28*(3), 447–467.
European Council. Directive 2001/55/EC of 20 July 2001 on minimum standards for giving temporary protection in the event of a mass influx of displaced persons and on measures promoting a balance of efforts between Member States in receiving such persons and bearing the consequences thereof. *OJ L 212*, 7 August 2001, p. 12–23.
Goldner Lang, I. (2022). Intra-EU mobility of EU citizens and third-country nationals where EU free movement and migration policies intersect or disconnect? In P. de Bruycker & E. (Lilian) Tsourdi (Eds.), *Research handbook on EU migration and asylum law*. Edward Elgar.
Milazzo, E. (2023). *Refugee protection and solidarity*. Oxford University Press.
Phuong, C. (2003). Enlarging 'Fortress Europe': EU accession, asylum, and immigration in candidate countries. *The International and Comparative Law Quarterly, 52*(3), 641–663.
Sandler, T. (1977). Impurity of defense: an application to the economics of alliances. *Kyklos, 30*(3), 443–460.
Sandler, T., & Forbes, J. F. (1980). Burden-sharing, strategy, and the design of NATO. *Economic Enquiry, 18*(3), 425–444.
Schimmelfennig, F. (2021). Rebordering Europe: external boundaries and integration in the European Union. *Journal of European Public Policy, 28*(3), 311–330.
Thym, D., & Tsourdi, E. (Lilian). (2017). Searching for solidarity in the EU asylum and border policies: Constitutional and operational dimensions. *Maastricht Journal of European and Comparative Law, 24*(5), 605–621.

CHAPTER 6

Poland: Nation-building, Populism, and Ethnicity

INTRODUCTION

With the fall of communism in 1989, Central-Eastern European (CEE) countries were affected by processes of change in their politics, economy, and society. The disintegration of the Soviet Union led to the re-conceptualisation of the economic and political systems of the post-Soviet countries. In this context, during the 1990s, the CEE region started to embrace the Western countries' neo-liberal system, not only from a socio-economic point of view, but also political through democratic elections. After the fall of communism and the 2004 accession to the EU, CEE countries began to experience a rise in populist political parties. In this process, their rise may be considered a reaction to the homogenisation of these societies partly as a result of the European integration project. These populist nationalistic waves affected important issues such as migration, the environment, and CEE-EU relations.

In the case of Poland, the political process (from communism to neo-liberalism) was led by a strong cohort of politicians that opposed the previous system, which led to the birth of the current political parties in the Sejm.[1] In recent years, the EU itself has experienced strong opposition from the Polish government to attempts to integrate certain policy areas,

[1] Lower house of the bicameral parliament of Poland.

© The Author(s), under exclusive license to Springer Nature Switzerland AG 2023
D. Caballero-Vélez, *Contesting Migration Crises in Central Eastern Europe*, Mobility & Politics,
https://doi.org/10.1007/978-3-031-44037-3_6

including migration and the environment (see Caballero-Vélez & Pachocka, 2021). However, there has been some visible contrasts. Despite the Polish government's previous 'closed door' policy, exercised in 2015 and 2021, in 2022, the Polish government decided to allow into the country most of the refugees coming from Ukraine. Important variables such as closeness in cultural values, historical roots, and religion may be important factors to understanding the Polish government's differing approach towards refugees, that is, Middle East in the earlier years and Ukrainian in the most recent. This chapter offers a comprehensive explanation of the Polish political system's evolution and clash of nation-identity formation to understand their influence on national migration policymaking. In this regard, it is important to clarify, on the one hand, the general identity of the state in question and, on the other hand, the identity envisioned by the ruling political party. In the following sections, the case of Polish identity is reviewed by showing how the current ruling political party (Law and Justice, PiS) and its idea of the Polish nation influences Polish migration policies and, in this case, the perception of public goods provision. Based on extracts of interviews with Polish experts on migration, I offer a political-identity approach to understanding the Polish government's categorisation of different types of migration governance and the interpretation of the costs and benefits of providing refugee protection. Then, I demonstrate the significance of 'otherness' to help understand the interpretation of costs and benefits of different migration governance frameworks, in this case, the refugee regime.

The Polish Party System and its Evolution Since 1989

Poland's political history since WWII was greatly marked by the Soviet Union's control of the system. Even if the country was technically an independent state from the Soviet Union, the socialist (i.e., communist) Polish United Workers' Party (*Polska Zjednoczona Partia Robotnicza*, PZPR) ruled Poland until the 1980s. In 1952, Poland became the Polish People's Republic (PRL), and after Stalin's death in 1953, the country started a period of changes in terms of liberties. The PRL, with its one-party system under Soviet influence, had to contend with numerous internal social movements and civil demonstrations demanding democratic changes.

By the end of the 1980s, along with economic crises, there was mass opposition against the PZPR. In 1989, this opposition represented by the famed trade union federation, Solidarity (*Solidarność*), carried out the Round Table negotiations with the PZPR leadership with the objective of holding free elections (Van Kessel, 2015). Solidarity's victory in the subsequent voting was the first step towards the end of communism in Poland and the beginning of a systematic transformation that would include market reforms, social transformation, and democratisation, all marked by volatility in the political system. If the concept of state-nation building is taken as understanding the recent conceptualisation of the Polish nation, the period of Solidarity marked a turning point in the building of the Polish identity as a European one (O'Neal, 2017)—an idea in opposition to the concepts of Polishness proffered by populist political parties of the future.

During the 1990s, the Polish political scene was characterised by a weak party system. This was in part due to the split of Solidarity into numerous political forces. The presence of the Democratic Left Alliance (*Sojusz Lewicy Demokratycznej*, SLD) formed by former communist politicians from the PZPR led to a divided Sejm in the 1991 and 1993 political elections. Nevertheless, the 1993 elections marked the beginning of the integration of political parties into coalitions of parties. This was the result of a change in electoral law that introduced an electoral threshold of 5% for parties and 8% for coalitions to enter into the Sejm. While post-Solidarity political parties needed to form coalitions, SLD for a long time remained a consistently large bloc. In 1993, the SLD formed a coalition government with the Polish Peasant Party (*Polskie Stronnictwo Ludowe*, PSL), resulting in victory for their candidate for the presidency, the social democrat Aleksander Kwaśniewski. This event consolidated the former communist politicians in power (Van Kessel, 2015). In this regard, Wróbel (2011) reflects on how the post-Solidarity camp divisions built up the future Polish party system: on the one hand, there were those who wanted to carry out the democratisation process without looking at the past, but, on the other hand, there were others who did not want the participation of the former communist politicians. This division in building the new political scenario would be fundamental to the future split between the populist and establishment political parties.

In 1997, a new right-centre alliance formed by the parties and groups descendant from Solidarity and Solidarity itself, Solidarity Electoral Action (*Akcja Wyborcza*, AWS) won the elections. Consequently, AWS formed a parliamentary coalition with the neo-liberal political party, Freedom Union (*Unia Wolności*, UW). Internal conflicts between AWS and UW resulted in the subsequent formation of different political groups. In 2001, among these different political groups was Civic Platform (*Platforma Obywatelska*, PO) and Law and Justice (*Prawo i Sprawiedliwość*, PiS). That same year, the SLD (the successor of the old communist party, PZPR) won the elections in coalition with the Polish Peasant Party (*Polskie Stronnictwo Ludowe*, PSL); some scandals involving alleged corruption damaged the image of the government, resulting in support in the polls shifting to PO and PiS (Szczerbiak, 2007).

Polish Ruling Political Parties (2004–2020): The Birth of the Two-Party System

As shown in Table 7.1, in the 2005 elections, SLD lost seats in the Sejm, while PO and PiS became the two main political parties in Poland. The rise of these two political parties marked the birth of a new era in the Polish political landscape in which the volatility that used to mark the Sejm in the 1990s was replaced by a two-party system in which two visions of Poland would be represented: PO, representing the liberal establishment political position in the Sejm, and PiS, with an anti-establishment radical discourse. Although both political parties shared a past in Solidarity, PO was characterised as an anti-populist party while PiS kept up the tradition of Solidarity-style populism. Accordingly, after 2005, PiS started its transformation from elitism to populism, for instance, 'employing the slogan "Close to the People"' (Kucharczyk & Wysocka, 2008, p. 79, as cited in Van Kessel, 2015).

While the SLD did not have much competition during the 1990s and beginning of the 2000s, it dropped in the 2005 elections. That year marked the beginning of a change of power between PiS and PO. In 2005, PiS won the presidency and the parliamentary elections, forming a coalition with two radical parties of the same self- identified Catholic values and 'Euroscepticist spirit'—Self-Defence(*Samoobrona Odrodzenie*, SO),[2]

---

[2] In 2007, SO was founded by groups that split from the political party Self-Defence of the Republic of Poland (*Samoobrona Rzeczpospolitej Polskiej*, SRP). The SRP is a 'radical organisation of Polish farmers, since 2001 a catch-all party that voiced strong objections to the policies of all post-1989 governments and questioned the conditions of Poland's entry to the EU' (Jasiewicz & Jasiewicz-Betkiewicz, 2005, p. 1106)

and League of Polish Families(*Liga Polskich Rodzin*, LPR).[3] Due to numerous disputes with the two minor parties in the coalition, the PiS government was unstable (Szczerbiak, 2007, as cited in Van Kessel, 2015). In 2007, after a PO victory in the elections (41.5%) in coalition with PSL, PiS (32.1%) passed into the opposition (Van Kessel, 2015). In addition, LPR and SO did not gain any seats in the Sejm, disappearing from the Polish political landscape. Furthermore, during these elections, the social democrats obtained 13.2% (Van Kessel, 2015). These elections may be considered as the point of the establishment of a two-party system in Poland. In May 2015, PiS won the presidency after having secured parliamentary majority in the elections (Fomina & Kucharczyk, 2016)

THE RISE OF NATIONAL-CONSERVATIVE POPULISM IN POLAND

Recently, much literature on populism in Europe has sought to understand the dynamics of the phenomenon beyond the rise of populist movements and their characteristics. In the case of Poland, Fomina and Kucharczyk (2016) point out that PiS belongs to the category of 'contemporary authoritarian populism', and according to Pippa Norris (2019), this form of populism is not driven by economics.[4] Hence, identity politics is fundamental to understanding the extent to which PiS has gained votes by reconceptualising the concept of the Polish nation.

In defining the national identity, it is important to look at nation-state building literature. A growing amount of literature is devoted to understanding states' democratisation processes through a nation-building perspective. Nevertheless, scholars doubt whether it is necessary to analyse both processes—the 'nation' and 'state'—in a separate way, as reflected in some literature (e.g., Wimmer & Schille, 2002). While nationalism and populism have been discussed separately in the literature, in recent years, some scholars have attempted to show populist dynamics through theoretical approaches to analysis of nationalism (see Brubaker, 2010). For instance, Müller (2016) reflects on how current populist rhetoric combines both anti-elitism and what its adherents view is a superior notion of

---

[3] A conservative and Catholic political party founded in 2001. It used anti-EU rhetoric in the 2005 electoral campaign (Jasiewicz & Jasiewicz-Betkiewicz, 2005).

[4] Economics may be considered as a factor in PiS rise but not the only one, for instance, PiS gained much popularity by opting for increased social transfers.

a true citizen of a nation, refusing any kind of element that opposes this idea. The formulation of national politics may shape the vision of the nation enhanced by the government in power (Caballero-Vélez & Misiuna, 2022). Building on this idea, Grotenhuis (2016) notes that nation-building processes and national identity rhetoric are based on the premise and notion of homogeneity.

Poland's Identity: Law and Justice's 'Re-vision' of the Polish Nation

In the case of the Visegrad countries (Czechia, Hungary, Poland, and Slovakia), the nation-building process may be reflected in the rise of nationalist populist political parties trying to re-conceptualise the nation (Slavish identities, Catholicism, etc.). In the Polish case, O'Neal (2017, p. 2) claims that 'what is happening in Poland is a collision of two state-building projects, based upon fundamentally incompatible narratives about Polish identity'. Despite the ethnic heterogeneity from the past, its transformation towards a homogeneous nation-state (see Caballero-Vélez & Misiuna, 2022) has led both PiS and PO to have built two completely different concepts of Poland as a nation and Polish people as a society. Some of the characteristics of the PiS idea of Poland and the party as a national-conservative populist movement include the view that (Krzyżanowski, 2018):

- Poland's main religion is Catholicism;
- Polish national values are based on Catholic values;
- Poland has a glorious past (e.g., the period of the Kingdom of Poland) and historical enemies (e.g., communism, foreign forces);
- Poland has Slavic roots, reinforced by relationships with Eastern countries such as Ukraine;
- The EU is a threat to Polish sovereignty and Brussels is a foreign force that wrongfully attempts to command Polish domestic politics;
- EU values are incompatible with Poland's values and historically, that the Western European vision of political reality is different from the one in Central-Eastern European countries.

There is some indication that Law and Justice's idea of a 'true' Pole may be represented by individual identification with its idea of a Polish nation, as mentioned by EX3: *'the official rhetoric is that you can be a Polish citizen but not a member of the Polish nation because Polish nation must be Catholic, Roman Catholic (...)*' (EX3 interview). In addition, the following quote illustrates the concept of 'pertaining to the Polish nation' represented in some legal documents such as the Karta Polaka (Pole's Card): '*this special document for Poles who were born outside Poland but have, for example, a Polish grandfather or grandmother, it means that they don't have Polish citizenship but they are part of the Polish nation. If they get this Polish card, for example, they have access to the labour market, access to school and so and so on, even if they don't have Polish citizenship*' (EX3, interview). A nation itself is not born in a vacuum, it is shaped by many factors such as political ideologies, and nationalistic political parties tend to frame their discourses to stress the homogeneity of the nation (Caballero-Vélez & Misiuna, 2022). This empirical evidence in the statement 'member of the nation' reflects the separation of both the state and nation concepts by calling into question the extent to which PiS attempts to re-conceptualise or build anew the Polish idea of nation based on the party adherents' own assumption of what 'Polishness' is.

The Identity of the 'Other': European Identity vs. Polish Identity

One cannot understand Law and Justice's current politics and vision of political reality without understanding the process of the formation of such an idea. In the case of Polish identity, O'Neal (2017) puts the emphasis on the concept of the 'other', noting that 'ideas of the "other" are an indispensable aid in helping to define what the nation is, by comparison to what it is not' (p. 3). Identifying an agent's identity is a complex task. Through a brief explanation of recent Polish politics, I have sought to give an overview about how the Law and Justice party understands political reality and how this vision shapes domestic migration policy. By identifying the process of identity formation, Roberts (2016) refers to 'altercasting', a process of an agent's self- identification by declaring other agents' identities. On this subject, Campbell claims that the agents solidify their own identities through interaction with other agents and establishing a 'them' and an 'us' (Campbell, 1988).

Law and Justice's identity in migration matters may be exemplified by how this political party perceives the EU. Although the majority of Poles accepted entering the EU and party itself accepted Poland's accession, PiS has always refused the idea of the EU as a superior hierarchical institution that promotes different values to its idea of the Polish nation, as EX3 stated: '*80% of Poles accept our membership of the European Union because for us, it is absolutely crucial in many aspects, from many different aspects. (...), from a hierarchical point of view it is very difficult for him (Jarosław Kaczyński),[5] to accept any orders from the European Commission, European Parliament, etc; but, on the other hand, he has to accept it because the place of Poland is inside the European Union, not outside the European Union*' (EX3, interview). This brings us to the question of how Law and Justice seeks to promote a kind of 'Polishness' that is not compatible with the EU's, resulting in a formulation of national policy by which Poland's interests come first. Defining Law and Justice's identity by analysing its relationship with the EU must be carefully considered. By the assumptions claimed before, it is important to point out that PiS does not form its identity by its relationship with the EU, rather that it serves as a mirror for understanding how Law and Justice 'is' or 'is not'—in Kubálková's words (2001), 'states create each other as enemies, rivals, or partners and proceed to share their interpretations of their respective identities' (Kubálková, 2001, as cited in Roberts, 2016, p. 54). If Law and Justice's identity process is compared with Civic Platform's, one can perceive two completely different visions of Poland: '*a Civic version, promoted by the mainstream post-Solidarity elite, permits the European identity to reinforce or complement Polishness; and a neo- traditional version, sponsored by PiS and the national-populist right, rejects as deluded or treacherous the embrace of a separate European identity*' (O'Neal, 2017, p. 2). The clash of these two visions represented by Civic Platform and Law and Justice shows us how Poland's relationship with the EU has changed over the past decade. Thus, EX6 refers to how PiS attempts to re-generate some feelings from before Poland's accession to the EU: '*(...) Before Poland was joining the EU, the society was not kind of allowed to say that they had some feelings (...), because we are modern, we are in the EU, these politicians, PiS, they saw this need and they managed to kind of re-generate these feelings (...), our old feelings vs. EU feelings, that we have our feelings but the EU also wants to put their feelings (on us)*' (EX6, interview).

As mentioned above, Law and Justice formulates the narrative of the 'other', the West seeking to control Poland's interests, and this vision influences the formulation of its own national policies (O'Neal, 2017). For instance, in the case of the 2015 Relocation Scheme, initiated at the EU level, one respondent expressed the following: '*these Visegrad

[5] Chairman of Law and Justice.

countries, these countries cooperating together or having similar attitudes to this, I mean all of them, except Slovakia alone, they didn't do any action about the relocation, so they infringe the agreement' (EX1 interview). Whereas for Law and Justice, the EU represents Western ideas not compatible with Polish traditions, cooperating with Visegrad Group (V4) countries might be more compatible with PiS's traditional values, and in this case, 'the conservative narrative delegitimises the version of Polish nationalism that is fused with a European identity by implying that it is not really Polish, but instead the slavish emulation of the "alien" norms of the EU' (O'Neal, 2017, p. 2). Cooperation with V4 counties in European politics highlights the importance of the identification of a common CEE region identity among these countries. Despite common cultural trends and geographical proximity, all these countries share another important element: they all have passed through the transition from the communist regime to the western bloc and, on the basis of this, the post-Cold War period might be seen as a period of identity building (Kazharski, 2018). By adopting the notion of 'altercasting', one may argue that Law and Justice refuses the idea of full identification with the Western European identity. In this identity-building process, V4 countries are reluctant to be seen as foreigners in the EU but, at the same time, commonly refuse what they view as the imposition of Western European traditions.

The 2015 migration-management crisis served as a catalyst to put a manifest and normative gap between Central European countries such as Germany and the governments of the CEE Member States (Kazharski, 2018). The German government, lead then by Chancellor Angela Merkel, decided to take a humanitarian approach to accepting Middle Eastern refugees (Kazharski, 2018); polar opposite to that was the V4 approach to the crisis, which was completely securitised. This dual approach serves as an example of the broadly different approaches taken by the majority of the Member States. In recent years, numerous populist and Eurosceptic movements and political parties in Europe have used migration as a tool of self-identification by contrasting their view against the EU's, portrayed as a singular entity. In Poland's case, Law and Justice has viewed EU attempts to shape national migration politics in general and relocate refugees in particular as a kind of imposition of values and identity.

The 2014 conflict in Crimea provoked an increased number of asylum applications from Ukraine. This situation led the Polish government to be better prepared for the asylum crisis when the 2015 migration-management crisis started: '*Before, when the war in Ukraine started, then we were preparing plans about what to do in case Ukraine inflows were massive ..., there were more security measures and also reception measures, how to accommodate, you know, how to provide social assistance to this possible group, so it was, in my opinion, in my perception, it was a more serious time for preparing some measures than in 2015, than the migration crisis alone*' (EX2, interview). In 2014, Civic Platform was the ruling political party and the Polish national asylum system had started to be reinforced. In 2015, Law and Justice took power and almost immediately adopted a different approach to the refugee migration crisis, as EX3 outlines: '*Until 2015, before the migration crisis, I think we had had in the European Union, also in Poland, a liberal point of view on migration, especially labour migration. But I think that since the migration crisis, it has changed everything. Now, we have two different approaches to migration: on the one hand, a lot of politicians are still calling for keep the borders open for migrants; but, on the other hand, the society is also against it, especially if we take into account the (type of) refugees*' (EX3, interview). One interpretation of this would be that the shift in the Polish government changed society's attitudes towards migration in general, and, refugees in particular. Although there were not significant legal changes in Polish national asylum law, Law and Justice opposed firmly the Relocation Scheme, changing Poland's' position in the framework of EU policymaking: '*this Council about the Relocation Scheme and the 1st of September, if I remember, in 2015, the Polish government decided to take part in the Relocation Scheme, but a few months later, after taking power, Law and Justice, the new government, blocked it and said 'no, we don't want to welcome any refugees from Syria, Lebanon or other countries, especially from Libya and Syria*' (EX3, interview). Thus, the Polish government increased border control, as EX7 recalls: '*there were restrictive controls on the borders. It was a problem strictly connected with the migration crisis, rather than the long-standing traditional kind with crossing and the Polish border guard*' (EX7, interview). The massive influx of migrants was perceived negatively by the Polish government; in addition, the terrorist attacks in Brussels and Paris marked a point of no return for the government to maintain its strategy of not relocating these refugees. In his interview, EX5 also pointed out the poor level of preparedness in facing such a challenge: '*the situation was like really unexpected although I was a bit surprised because ..., of the risk analysis that should be done like properly for at least 15 years and then suddenly it appeared like in 2015 even with "hello we have this overload of people coming through Europe and we have no tools to deal with it"* (EX5 interview).

This sheds light on the Polish government's conception of its identity and also on how this view influenced, in the case of Relocation Scheme, the authorities' attitudes towards Syrian asylum-seekers. On the other hand, as stated earlier, interviewees mentioned the still open door to Ukrainian refugees during the 2014 conflict in Crimea. In the interviews, there were some interesting mentions about what would be the government's position to a possible influx of forced migrants from Belarus (Belarusians). In this case, Poland would extend the open-door policy to them, by which international protection would be granted to Belarusian asylum-seekers.

POLISH NATION-BUILDING PROJECTS AND MIGRATION POLICIES

The EU refugee Relocation Scheme was seen by Law and Justice as an EU imposition on Poland and considered it as a threat to national sovereignty, as EX1 saw it: '*with this programme, the EU was treated as 'you', a strange body who doesn't have (the right) to tell us what our independent country will do (...), so they did this (and it was) a very big problem, and there is an explanation to say that the 'EU will not tell us what we should do*" (EX1, interview). Previous studies on migration have suggested the innate public goods characteristic of different types of migration governance. Research in this area has been limited to theoretical explanations of political scenarios in which the migration phenomena occurred or are used to explain the rationale behind states enhancing some migration policies. Nevertheless, from a collective action and public goods theory perspective, there has been as yet no empirical examination of states' preferences in a situation of different political choices regarding migration. In addition, although much important work has been carried out on agents' actions from a rationalist public goods perspective, little attention has been paid to the constructivist nature of public goods provision. When it comes to the selection of a case study, a detailed examination of Law and Justice's perceptions towards migration reveals that its opposition to the EU's attempts to instil a major, integrated CEAS is contrary to its vision of migration through a labour lens, most of it, from Central-Eastern European countries, as was expressed by one interviewee: '*until 2015, before the migration crisis, I think we had had in the European Union, also in Poland, a liberal point of view on migration, especially labour migration.*

But I think that since the migration crisis, it has changed everything. Now we have two different approaches to migration: on the one hand, a lot of politicians are still calling for keep the borders open for migrants; but, on the other hand, the society is also against it, especially if we take into account the (type of) refugees' (EX3, interview). Hence, Law and Justice's perceptions towards migration is determined by the agent's social dimension built on identity and norms, being part of its idea of the Polish nation. The identity is marked by a notion of the EU as the 'other', an entity imposing its own identity through, in this research case, migration legal measures. That social dimension determines agents' selection of choices in a particular situation. In the case of Poland, the ruling political party's own identity plays a crucial role in determining policies. When it comes to migration policy, identity may shape different perceptions of different groups of migrants. The interview above demonstrates clearly the attempt of reformulation by the Polish government of the concept of the Polish nation, an idea framed by the construction of a kind of Polish reality characterised by certain values, traditions, history, and so on. This construction of reality determines Law and Justice's actions in a given situation (social dimension), as we can observe in the following Diagram 6.1:

Diagram 6.1 serves to illustrate how Law and Justice's (as an agent in the dimension of action) perception of reality is determined by its identity. In other words, Law and Justice's view of itself determines its vision of the Polish nation and this in turn influences its choices in various scenarios. To this extent, the idea of the Polish nation is a social construct within the political party's identity. If we use this constructivist rationale in order to understand the formulation of migration policies and specifically the perceptions towards migration, one may argue that the Law and Justice party may formulate migration policies according to its own vision of Poland, as shown in Diagram 6.2:

As is evident from Diagram 6.2, Law and Justice formulates its migration policy by its perception of the Polish nation (its reality). When it comes to making a decision about migration, this perception of reality constructs a determined vision of how national migration policy should be set. In addition, the social dimension has, in part, an influence on Law and Justice's migration policy choices. It is important to point out that the social dimension is based on norms, rules, institutions, and so on, and that actors act, to some extent, in accordance with this, but even though the actor's identity determines its behaviour in a certain social situation, as Roberts (2016) claims, 'the agent's identity in the situation of choice

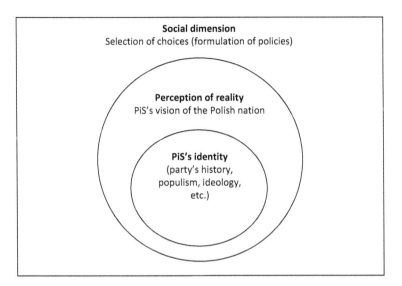

Diagram 6.1 Law and Justice's dimension of action. (Source: Own elaboration)

determines the agent's appropriateness' (p. 17). For a more detailed examination of what has been discussed above, the next section analyses the empirical part of the appropriateness rationale behind the actor's decisions. This becomes clear when one examines the case of PiS in its approach towards migration policy. If we take into consideration the 2015 Relocation Scheme,[6] despite the Member States' obligations towards the relocation of refugees, Poland's position was contrary to it. Within the framework of this case, one may argue that EU institutions provide a set of norms, rules, and so on, by which the Member States should shape their preferences and adapt themselves to this institutional dimension. Accordingly, in a situation in which 'when the agent asks, 'what kind of agent am I?' the agent is not asking about its internal characteristics such as personality, it is asking about what kind of agent it is relative to the social setting' (Sending, 2002, p. 489 as cited in Roberts, 2016, p. 17). Poland's ruling party interpreted the situation as, while there is a migration crisis, the EU is enforcing its norms-obligations on the Member States from its own perception of reality, interpreting the situation according to its own preferences and determined by its identity, while Law and Justice's concept of reality determined

[6] It is analysed in more detail in Chap. 5.

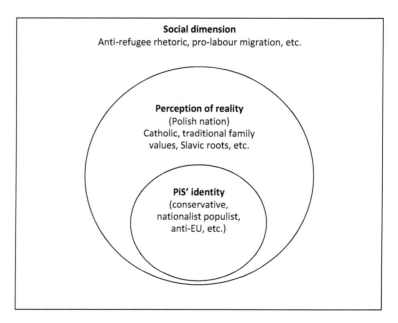

Diagram 6.2 Law and Justice's dimension of action (migration case). (Source: Own elaboration)

how it would behave in a situation in which a massive influx of migrants coming from the Middle East were supposed to be relocated among the Member States.

Conclusions

If we take into consideration the PiS construction of reality (Catholic, traditional family values, Eurosceptic, etc.), it is not surprising then to claim that the appropriate behaviour for the Polish party in power was not to relocate any of these refugees to its own territory even if mandated by the EU. In this regard, the identification of the EU as the 'other' influenced the Law and Justice's maximisation of utility to decide not to relocate the refugees. In the context of the 2015 refugee crisis in which the EU is seen as an external agent that seeks to impose its own values and/or identity on Poland, Law and Justice's identity formulated as the opposite influenced its costs-benefits calculation. In this case, if the EU reflects how important is to relocate these Middle Eastern migrants, Law and Justice viewed the cost of it as higher, because its identity is opposite to the EU's. By this 'altercasting' process, one may assume how Law and Justice's identity influences its utility in taking actions on migration issues.

From a constructivist identity-utility model, the justification for the assumption that Law and Justice decided not to relocate refugees is given by its interpretation of the costs and benefits. In the case of 2015 Relocation Scheme, Law and Justice, in a subjective way, reflected on the costs and benefits of relocating the refugees. To this extent, this research assumes that the subjective interpretation of having more costs than benefits in the choice of relocating refugees is a result of the political party's concept of reality built on its partisan identity. In the case of the 2015 Relocation Scheme, one of the main reasons some Central-Eastern EU Member States expressed reluctance to the programme was fear for security (Caballero-Vélez & Pachocka, 2019). This brings us to the question of how an agent's identity influences its construction of potential costs and benefits, and in this case, security may be seen by the Polish ruling party as a high cost of relocating refugees. In the case of Germany, for instance, it was the opposite; Germany had a different position to Poland's regarding asylum-seeker burden-sharing (Caballero-Vélez & Pachocka, 2019). Refugee protection governance may be considered as a public good, and consequently 'the security threat to each state may be considered a private cost' (Caballero-Vélez & Pachocka, 2021, p. 6). Despite studies of the possible costs and benefits of the provision of refugees (see Betts, 2003), there has remained a need to demonstrate it through empirical evidence. In the next section, the costs and benefits of labour and forced migration governance can be estimated by framing Law and Justice's narrative towards migration.

REFERENCES

Betts, A. (2003). Public goods theory and the provision of refugee protection: The role of the joint-product model in burden-sharing theory. *Journal of Refugee Studies, 16*(3), 274–296.

Brubaker, R. (2010). Migration, membership, and the modern nation-state: Internal and external dimensions of the politics of belonging. *Journal of Interdisciplinary History, 41*(1), 61–78.

Caballero-Vélez, D., & Misiuna, J. (2022). When exit policies determine entry policies: The case of the *Karta Polaka*. *International Migration*, Special Issue. https://doi.org/10.1111/imig.13050

Caballero-Vélez, D., & Pachocka, M. (2019). Understanding EU Member States cooperation within the asylum regime during the migration and refugee crisis from an IR perspective. In Adamczyk, A., Dziembała, M., Kłos, A., Pachocka, M.(eds.), *EU facing current challenges, opportunities, crisis and conflicts*. Warsaw: Elipsa.

Caballero-Vélez, D., & Pachocka, M. (2021). Producing public goods in the EU: European integration processes in the fields of refugee protection and climate stability. *European Politics and Society, 22*(1), 1–18.

Campbell, D. (1988). *Writing security: United States foreign policy and the politics of identity* (Revised Edn). University of Minnesota Press.

Fomina, J., & Kucharczyk, J. (2016). Populism and protest in Poland. *Journal of Democracy, 27*(4), 58–68.

Grotenhuis, R. (2016). *Nation-building as necessary effort in fragile states*. Amsterdam University Press.

Jasiewicz, K., & Jasiewicz-Betkiewicz, A. (2005). Poland. *European Journal of Political Research, 44*(7–8), 1106–1115.

Kazharski, A. (2018). The end of 'Central Europe'? The rise of the radical right and the contestation of identities in Slovakia and the Visegrad four. *Geopolitics, 23*(4), 754–780.

Krzyżanowski, M. (2018). Discursive shifts in ethno-nationalist politics: On politicization and mediatization of the 'Refugee Crisis' in Poland. *Journal of Immigrant and Refugee Studies, 16*(1–2), 76–96.

Kubálková, V. (2001). Foreign Policy, international politics, and constructivism. In V. Kubálková (Ed.), *Foreign policy in a constructed world* (pp. 15–37). M.E. Sharpe.

Kucharczyk, J., & Wysocka, O. (2008). Poland. In G. Mesežnikov, O. Gyárfášová, & D. Smilov (Eds.), *Populist politics and liberal democracy in Central and Eastern Europe* (pp. 71–100). Institute for Public Affairs.

Müller, J.-W. (2016). *What is populism?* University of Pennsylvania Press.

Norris, P. (2019). *Cultural backlash: Trump, Brexit, and authoritarian populism*. Cambridge University Press.

O'Neal, M. (2017). The European 'other' in Poland's conservative identity project. *The International Spectator, 52*(1), 28–45.

Roberts, J. C. (2016). Constructing the other: Forming identities through ascribed preferences. *Towson University Journal of International Affairs, 49*(2), 43–58.

Sending, O. J. (2002). Constitution, choice and change: Problems with the 'logic of appropriateness' and its use in constructivist theory. *European Journal of International Relations, 8*(4), 443–470.

Szczerbiak, A. (2007). Social Poland' defeats 'Liberal Poland'? The September–October 2005 Polish parliamentary and presidential elections. *Journal of Communist Studies and Transition Politics, 23*(2), 203–232.
Van Kessel, S. (2015). *Populist parties in Europe: Agents of discontent?* Palgrave Macmillan.
Wimmer, A., & Schille, N. G. (2002). Methodological nationalism and beyond: Nation-state building, migration and the social sciences. *Global Networks, 2*(4), 301–334.
Wróbel, S. (2011). Mourning populism. The case of Poland. *Polish Sociological Review, 176*(176), 437–456.

CHAPTER 7

Modelling Preferences towards Refugee Protection: The Polish Government Case

INTRODUCTION

The literature on refugee protection based on actors' cost-benefit rationales does not reveal comprehensive information about preference formation. A more realistic understanding of states' preferences towards refugee protection should not just look to the instrumentalist logic behind states' rationales, but also take into account that the benefits are shaped by identities, customs, and norms. The rationale choice approach fails in understanding, for instance, situations in which similar countries have different approaches to refugee protection or the same government may enhance policies differently towards groups of refugees.

Some scholars have attempted to understand how political contestation may shape actors' preferences in refugee protection: Thielemann (2003) argues the importance of the socio-cultural context to understanding states' motivations towards migration, and Betts (2003, p. 287) refers to 'inter-subjective norms within a given society'. Based on the constructivist approach, this chapter provides a model to understand how the Polish government constructs its various perceptions of the benefits of refugee protection. The main premise is that the benefits are perceived depending on a state's identity(ies) and norms. The point is surely that finding a purely empirical approach to constructivism is a difficult task. Contrary to the pure 'static' positive nature of other political science theories, such as rational choice, the subjectivity innate in a constructivist reality raises some questions about the research methodology to be used. By the same token, positivism does not reflect entirely the process of reality construction, and to some extent, is criticised by assuming that any dimension in the social sciences research inquiry process may be quantified. Accordingly, this chapter offers an analysis that employs a model to frame the security cost and humanitarian benefits of refugee protection. The main premise is that the Polish government enacts its policies in refugee protection according to the norms and customs of its identity (see Chap. 4). Notwithstanding humanitarian perceptions towards certain groups of refugees (in this case, Middle East refugees) results in an interpretation that providing international protection to this group of people is a risk to national security. On the other hand, other groups of migrants (e.g., from Eastern Europe) may be seen as deserving protection for humanitarian reasons. To conduct a frame analysis of both of the security and humanitarian narratives of the Polish government, I operationalise the model based on, (A) the Habermas model of migration framing (1993), and (B) Roberts' identity-utility model theoretical framework (2019). The first model is used to categorise migration from different perspectives (identity, moral-universal, and utilitarian). The second model serves this research as a theoretical roadmap to provide an alternative methodological and epistemological vision to public goods theory based on the role of the actor's identity and norms (migration policy as the fact; identity as the epistemological basis).

Framing Migration

Constructivist quality research focuses on the participant-observation-and-interview data-gathering method (Given, 2008). In the case of interview interaction, the construction of reality is made by the respondent and the interviewer, the interpretation of reality is a mutual process. In the case of the research presented in this book, we have observed how the respondents have answered questions by the interpretation of the reality of Polish migration policies and Law and Justice's partisan identity. The first empirical process is the collection of data and the formulation of hypotheses by, later formulating a theoretical framework or model (inductive approach). In the research presented, I first systemised the Polish government's approaches towards different groups of migrants (epistemology), and second, with the collected data I modelled the costs and benefits based on the rationalist logic of public goods theory (ontology) (Diagram 7.1):

In methodological terms, the importance of this research is in the innovative insight into the analysis of public goods provision as social construct

Diagram 7.1 The inductive process. (Source: Own elaboration)

processes. To achieve this, the content analysis postulates the proper method to validate the variables raised from the theoretical framework to study the case of migration, for instance, the security-humanitarian narrative dichotomy. The main attempt to employ content analysis is the identification of themes and compares them to see the different variances in the variables. The themes used have been qualitatively coded and then the codes quantified by cross-tabulation. Employing a mixed-method approach represents an innovative aspect in the study of migration policies, which, so far, has predominantly focused on qualitative analysis and public choice/goods theory that has focused on quantitative analysis. Framing is a useful methodological tool when it is applied to policy conflicts by which actors/parties perceive policy situations and policies in conflicting ways (Schön & Rein, 1994, p. 18).

The Habermas model (1993) frames migration to distinguish media and elite discourses on European integration (Helbling, 2014). The frames provided by the model (identity, moral-universal, and utilitarian) provides a structure that may be used to code inductively every argument used by the political parties to frame migration themes (Helbling, 2014, p. 24):

(1) *The identity-related frames* refer to ideas and values from a determined community. In the case of nationalistic frames, it is more related with the preservation of the homogenous society and restrictive boundaries to maintain national identity, which in this case are considered as important identity frames. On the other hand, the multicultural frames are related with an openness and exchange of cultural values, integration, and so on.

(2) *The moral-universal* frames are related with universal rights that are accepted by the whole society. The moral-universal has a

more global perspective, while the multicultural frames have a nation-state perspective.

(3) *The utilitarian frames* relate to the justification of a position by which actors obtain a goal or defend an interest. The economic frame treats arguments by which migration may contribute to the economic prosperity of a state. On the other hand, security includes topics referring to security issues, such as terrorism. The pragmatic refers to efficiency and legal aspects (Table 7.1).

These frames are influenced by the role that a political party has in a society, and more specifically, its vision of the social world. Political parties introduce their concerns and interests into their migration argumentation (see Helbling et al., 2010). From these assumptions, I consider that any political actor, and specifically, political parties' views on migration are influenced by their own perception of reality. Taking the notion that actors' identities and norms shape their own reality, the migration policy-making process constitutes the results of the interpretation of the governments' constructed realities. The Habermas model follows an actor-driven logic (Helbling, 2014); nevertheless, it lacks coherence as actors' identities may not be considered a separate unit of enquiry, independent of other inherent actors' values, interests, and concerns.

THE IDENTITY-UTILITY MODEL: FRAMING SECURITY AND HUMANITARIANISM

The identity-utility model employed assumes that the provision of public goods is determined by actors' identities and norms. To frame identity is a complex task, the increase or decrease in utility depends on actors' perceptions of the costs and benefits. Based on Lutz and Caballero-Vélez (2023), the identification of, among others, *development, security,* and *reputation* as benefits and *security* as a cost, I frame development, reputation, and security following the Habermas utility (security and economy) and humanitarian protection frames:

(a) The economic contribution sub-frame represents the *development benefit*. In this case, refugees may be seen as a potential resource of economic growth and even framed as economic migrants.

Table 7.1 Habermas framing model

Types by Habermas	Identity		Moral-universal		Utilitarian			
Frame categories	Nationalistic	Multicultural	Moral-Universal	Economic	Labour and social security	Security	Pragmatic
Examples	Foreign infiltration National identity Loss of traditions Avoid Islamisation Avoid flows of refugees National sovereignty	European identity Advantages of cultural diversity Tolerance between religious groups Integration through tolerance	Fairness Equality Discrimination of groups Human Rights Freedom of opinion Geneva Convention Rule of law Democracy	Attract high-skilled immigrants Productivity International competition	Unemployment rates Salary dumping Poverty Welfare state Congestion social security system	Terrorism Youth criminality Internal security Political stability Organised crime	In our interest Capacity to act Legal security Reputation Legality Response to globalisation

Source: Helbling (2014, p 25), Elaborated from Habermas (1993)

(b) The humanitarian protection sub-frame refers to the *reputation benefit*. By giving international protection to asylum seekers, it is presumed to be a multicultural approach by the political party in question. By fulfilling humanitarian international law, the ruling political party expects an increase in prestige at the international level by fulfilling humanitarian international law.

(c) The securitisation of the migration sub-frame refers to the security benefit. A nationalistic frame is used by political parties using a narrative such as the threat of terrorism or crime, or need for border control (Table 7.2).

Each sub-frame has different categories or sub-groups to identify the specific variables. Type of migrants identifies the political party's perception of migrants without taking into consideration its real status. Accordingly, for instance, the ruling political party may perceive migrants as economic contributors, refugees, or terrorists. Depending on the frame used, the narrative towards them will be more nationalistic or more multicultural. The role of the state encompasses the state's legal (or not legal) commitments towards migrants. In the case of enhancing a multicultural frame, it will perceive rhetoric towards the compromise of respecting humanitarian law, respecting human rights, legality, burden-sharing, and coordination among states. The role of the state in securitisation emphasises what political commitments the state enhances in case migration is seen as a security problem, for instance, a national response, anti-EU rhetoric, and questions of

Table 7.2 Identity-utility model frames in migration

Frames	Multicultural		Nationalistic
Sub-frames	Economic contribution (development benefit)	Humanitarian protection (prestige benefit)	Securitisation of migration (security benefit)
Categories	Type of migrants Role of the state Same religion Similar cultural values	Type of migrants Role of the state Same religion Similar cultural values	Type of migrants Role of the state Religion Cultural values Defence Foreign infiltration

Note: The indicators of the categories are shown in the Appendix
Source: Own elaboration

sovereignty. Religion and cultural values differ depending on the frame. When it comes to a multicultural frame, a political party will refer to similarities in religion, culture, traditions, or historical roots. By the same token, in the case of using a nationalistic frame and seeing migrants as a security issue, religion and cultural values make a difference, as the state may see migrants with a different religion, in this case frequently Islam, and with traditions perceived as far from one's own as portending difficulties in integration. In the case of the securitisation of migration sub-frame, I have included two more categories: defence and foreign infiltration. While they may appear to be/seem the same, I have divided the concept of security into the defence category (e.g., internal security, political stability, and threat perception), and foreign infiltration as a category of a specific perceived threat (which typically includes rhetoric like 'invasion', 'Islam', 'Muslim'). The two categories are interconnected, nevertheless, separately they give us more information about the perception of the threat itself.

THE IDENTITY UTILITY MODEL: THE POLISH CASE

In the context of the EU migration-management crisis and migration and asylum policy in general, it has been shown how Law and Justice identifies the EU as the 'other'. The EU is seen by PiS as a foreign power seeking to impose its own vision of migration policy on the nation. Law and Justice's vision of 'Polishness' differs to the EU's self-identity:

- Law and Justice's idea of the Polish nation is highly related to ideals of states in the Visegrad region and identification with the Central Eastern European (CEE) region. The multicultural frame would be compared to Law and Justice's self-identification of its idea of Poland, which it sees as very close to Eastern European values, as reflected in its position as the ruling party towards the 2015 Refugee Relocation Scheme (see Chap. 4).
- Law and Justice's opposition to European identity and European values on migration reflects the idea of 'Polishness' that is incompatible with EU attempts to 'impose' a European identity. The nationalistic frame for migrants would be related with Law and Justice's identification as an anti-EU political party (Table 7.3).

This model offers interesting insight into Law and Justice's perceptions of different groups of migrants (Eastern European v. Middle Eastern).

Table 7.3 Identity-utility model for Law and Justice

Frames	Multicultural (Law and Justice: self-identification with V4 countries, CEE region, and Polishness)		Nationalistic (identification of the EU as the 'other')
Sub-frames	Economic contribution	Humanitarian protection	Securitisation of migration
Categories	Type of migrants Role of the state Same religion Similar cultural values	Type of migrants Role of the state Same religion Similar cultural values	Type of migrants Role of the state Religion Cultural values Defence Foreign infiltration

Note: The indicators of the categories are shown in the Appendix
Source: Own elaboration

The purpose for the selection of these groups of migrants is two-fold: (1) to compare and contrast the different perceptions of these groups according to the similarities and differences in Law and Justice's idea of the Polish nation, and (2) to see how refugee protection benefits are framed.

Framing Benefits and Costs

When it comes to framing costs and benefits and linking the public goods theoretical framework with attitudes towards migration, I propose a frame model that combines the Habermas typology and utility-identity rationale of providing public goods. For the purpose of this research, two types of migration are analysed through public goods theory: forced migration and labour migration (see Table 7.4).

By providing refugee protection, Poland may gain international prestige at the EU and international levels. If an EU Member State decides not to relocate refugees because of a perception of them as a security threat, other Member States may benefit from this public good in terms of political stability and security in EU territory. At the same time, the Polish government may obtain development gains such as economic growth. Perceptions may (or may not) be related with the real status and/or condition of the migrants. An asylum seeker who requests international protection, that is, refugee status, also may be perceived as an economic resource. In the Polish case, these perceptions are shaped by Law and

Table 7.4 The identity-utility model in refugee protection provision

Type of migration	Type of good	Benefits/Costs	Utility	Frames	
				Frames	Sub-frames
Forced migration (refugee protection)	Impure public good	Benefit International prestige	(+benefit/- cost)	Multicultural	Humanitarian protection
		Benefit Development	(+cost/- benefit)	Multicultural	Economic contribution
		Cost Security threat[a]	(+cost/- benefit)	Nationalistic	Securitisation of migration

[a]The benefits of goods provision are equivalent to the cost of the goods non-provision. Refugees may be perceived as a risk to national security, so as a cost; simultaneously, relocation, for example, may provide stability benefits in a given region (see Chap. 4)

Source: Own elaboration

Justice's positions towards migration in the context of the EU. Multicultural and nationalistic frames are derived from the Habermas identity frame, so, one may realise that the preference of gaining international recognition or protecting the nation and/or society against certain migrants will depend on the construction of the political actor's identity and norms

The Multicultural Frame: Prestige and Development Benefits

The frame used here is multicultural and the sub-frame is humanitarian protection, both referring to rhetoric related to integration, respecting humanitarian rights, and cultural similarities. The state expects to receive prestige and development benefits if refugees are relocated to its territory, or, in framing terms, when politicians' multicultural narrative is more employed than a nationalistic one (see Table 7.5). The model presented here provides an interesting starting point to see the variations in public goods- migration terms.

States may seek to relocate to their territory refugees with economic potential by investing in integration programmes and the welfare system. These economic 'costs' are equivalent to zero because the benefit of the refugees' economic contribution is much higher. Narratives such as cultural assimilation, access to education, and the health system are common in states that accept refugees. Political parties do not tend to separate

Table 7.5 The multicultural and nationalistic frames regarding prestige and security

Benefits/costs	International prestige (benefit)	Security threat (cost)
Frames	Multicultural	Nationalistic
Sub-frames	Humanitarian protection	Securitisation of migration

Source: Own elaboration

Table 7.6 The multicultural frame regarding development benefits

Benefits/costs	Development (benefit)	- (cost)
Frames	Multicultural	–
Sub-frames	Economic contribution	–

Source: Own elaboration

high- and low-skilled migrants, but view both as a unique group (Table 7.6).

If the cost of the security threat is higher than the benefits, security is constructed as the net benefit, so the scope will be to ensure protection to the nation and society. On this subject, the nationalistic frame is used by the political party more than the multicultural one. Speeches may include narratives like border control, terrorism, crime, and cultural differences (Table 7.7).

In the absence of the high frequency of use of the nationalistic frame, one may speculate about the security threat as a perceived cost and the benefits of enhancing security measures.

Conclusions

The international refugee regime has public goods characteristics. Refugee protection provides different types of benefits to host countries and also leads others to free-ride. Some governments enhance consistent refugee protection programmes due to labour shortages; in this case, refugees contribute to the labour demand. Despite the refugees' legal status, states may perceive asylum seekers as potential economic migrants. In refugee governance, burden-sharing problems arise when states enhance policies towards migrants from a security perspective, as the perceived security costs arise as a form of threat to the nation. Nevertheless, the security cost of not providing protection is equivalent to the net benefits that arise from

Table 7.7 The security public good frame

Good	Security public good	
Benefits/costs	International prestige (cost)	**Security (benefit)**
Frames	Multicultural	Nationalistic
Sub-frames	Humanitarian protection	Securitisation of migration

Source: Own elaboration

stability and political order in a certain region, and for this reason, states may tend to free-ride. Last but not least, states' identities may lead them to perceive refugees as victims that need international protection and that they have a moral duty to fulfil international humanitarian legal norms. Assuming that states act according to self-interest, this action normally is not 'altruistic' but rather motivated by perceived incentives, such as gaining international prestige.

The model provided by Habermas is useful to investigate politicians' narratives on migration issues. The model itself is a useful tool for later frames of the benefits that arise from providing international protection to refugees. The identity-utility model employed in the research operationalises refugee protection benefits and correlates it with the identity and norms dimensions of political actors. The model provides a background of comprehensive analysis for understanding political parties' rationales behind their migration policymaking processes. In the case of Poland, after having had solid analysis from interviews with experts about the current Poland-EU relationship and how it affects Polish national migration policies, the benefits and costs arise are made more visible in documents and politicians' speeches.

REFERENCES

Betts, A. (2003). Public goods theory and the provision of refugee protection: The role of the joint-product model in burden-sharing theory. *Journal of Refugee Studies, 3*, 274–296.

Given, L. M. (2008). *The SAGE encyclopedia of qualitative research methods*. Sage Publications.

Habermas, J. (1993). *Justification and application. Remarks on discourse ethics*. Polity Press.

Helbling, M. (2014). Framing immigration in Western Europe. *Journal of Ethnic and Migration Studies, 40*(1), 21–41.

Helbling, Marc, Dominic Höglinger, and Bruno Wüest. (2010). How Political Parties Frame European Integration. *European Journal of Political Research*, *49*(4), 495–521.

Lutz, P., & Caballero-Vélez, D. (2023). The public nature of refugee protection: What benefits for states? Paper presented at the Migration Policy Centre, Schuman Centre of Advanced Studies (European University Institute), Florence, IT, February 23.

Roberts, J. C. (2019). *Constructing global public goods*. Lexington Books.

Schön, D. A., & Rein, M. (1994). *Frame reflection*. Basic Books.

Thielemann, E. (2003). Between interests and norms: explaining burden-sharing in the European Union. *Journal of Refugee Studies, 16*(3), 253–273.

CHAPTER 8

Empirical Results: The (Non-) Provision of Refugee Protection

DATA AND CONTENT ANALYSIS

The period selected encompasses the years 2014–2019, when there were the Polish presidential elections (2014 and 2019), and major refugee crises in Europe (2015 and 2016). When it comes to the political situation in Poland, Law and Justice has been the ruling political party since 2015, which is an important factor. In 2014, the Crimea conflict led people from that region to leave and request international protection from some Member States, including Poland. Although it was a small number of applications, it is important to consider this event as a milestone in this research because it gives us some indicators about the Polish government's attitudes towards Eastern European refugees before the 2022 war in Ukraine. By the same token, the 2015 refugee crisis in Europe is considered another factor of interest in reviewing the perceptions towards Middle Eastern migrants. In 2015, the approbation of some legal measures by the EU regarding migration management were also key: the Refugee Relocation Scheme and the European Agenda on Migration, and Law and Justice's opposition to it. This study aims to provide information about the Polish government's attitudes towards Eastern European and Middle Eastern migrants before the 2021 and 2022 refugee crises. The response

© The Author(s), under exclusive license to Springer Nature Switzerland AG 2023
D. Caballero-Vélez, *Contesting Migration Crises in Central Eastern Europe*, Mobility & Politics,
https://doi.org/10.1007/978-3-031-44037-3_8

in both crises were completely different, and the rationale explored through the data analysis provides interesting insights into and predicts the Polish government's behaviour in those recent crises.

Apart from experts' interviews, which support the idea of the Polish government employing 'altercasting' with respect to the EU, the data selected to frame *development, international prestige,* and *security* include (A) parliamentary debates, (B), the political party's manifesto, and (C) political speeches and policy documents. To see how the ruling PiS's perceptions of Eastern European and Middle Eastern migrants differs, the time period selected is 2014–2019. The typology of the selected data for analysis is as follows: parliamentary debates regarding migration and asylum (in the years 2015, 2016, and 2017); speeches by then Prime Minister Beata Szydło (2016), Minister of the Interior Mariusz Blaszcz (2015, 2016, and 2017), and Minister of Foreign Affairs Witold Waszczykowski (2016 and 2017), as well as the 2019 Law and Justice electoral party manifesto. Frames with differing benefits are applied to the narratives towards Eastern European and Middle Eastern migrants. NVivo software was used for both the coding process and quantification of narrative frequencies. The coding process was based on gathering paragraphs/sentences related to themes in nodes,[1] as shown in the example in Table 8.1:

The paragraph above comes from Jarosław Kaczyński's speech in the Polish parliament. The statement fits the research questions formulated for this research. Once the qualitative coding process was conducted, a percentage for each frame is calculated as the total number of words coded across a determined frame in a document. In the case of the example in Table 8.1, of a total of 500 words coded in the file 'Parliamentary debate 2015' about Middle Eastern migrants, the file had 250 words coded in the node/frame called 'securitisation of migration' affiliated to Middle Eastern migrants, so the percentage of use of that frame regarding that group would be 50%. In order to get the percentages of use by nodes (e.g., securitisation of migration of Middle Eastern migrants) for specific data (e.g., Law and Justice's party manifesto), a cross-tabulation is displayed.[2] The row percentage displays the number of words coded as a percentage of

---

[1] In NVivo, nodes refer to codes, so a certain part of the material related to a theme is gathered under a pre-determined code.

[2] Columns contain the nodes; rows contain the files; cells contain the number of coding references at the intersection of a row and column.

8 EMPIRICAL RESULTS: THE (NON-) PROVISION OF REFUGEE PROTECTION

Table 8.1 Example of framing with NVivo software

Nodes	Paragraphs	Document	Coverage (%)
(1) Middle Eastern migrants (2) Nationalistic (3) Securitisation of migration (4) Role of the state	'namely, whether the government has the right under external pressure and without explicit consent from the people to make decisions that can have a high degree of negative impact on our lives, on our everyday life, on our public life, on our public space, on our real sphere of freedom, and finally, what was also raised here, on our safety'	Parliamentary debate 2015	0.17%

Source: Own elaboration

total words for the row. The column percentage displays the number of words as a percentage of total words for the column.

Row percentage (%)

	Multicultural (Node)	Nationalistic (Node)
Parliamentary debate 2015 (File)	17.1%	82.9%

Words coded (N)

	Multicultural (Node)	Nationalistic (Node)
Parliamentary debate 2015 (File)	159	771

By displaying the row percentage option, we may see the percentage of the node coded in that document. In the case of the 'multicultural' node, of the total words coded about Middle Eastern migrants in the 'Parliamentary debate 2015' document, 17.1% has a multicultural frame, or 159 words coded on that node. In the nationalistic frame, of the total words coded referring to Middle Eastern migrants in that file, this frame has a percentage of 82.9%, or 771 words coded. In order to employ graphics for a better understanding of the empirical part, I chose the percentage of use of the frequency numbers on Table 8.1 to show clearly that Law and Justice's Prime Minister, Minister of the Interior, and Foreign Minister use a security narrative to refer to Middle Eastern migrants and a multicultural one to refer to Eastern European migrants. Most significant is to see how little is said about Eastern European migrants (2.6%), for example, out of 2109 words coded, just 73 are related this group of migrants. The main reason for it probably is the scale of the refugee crisis in those years, so migration discussions were mainly focused on Middle Eastern migrants (2036 words coded out of a total of 2109).

For the graphic representation of the data analysis, I use the percentage of words coded. For instance, in Table 8.2:

- Of the total number of words coded in the document (1998), 2.8% were about Eastern European migrants and 97.2% were about Middle Eastern migrants.
- Of the words coded about Eastern European migrants, 100% fit the multicultural frame and none fit the nationalistic frame, so of the

Table 8.2 Matrix- frames frequency of use (PS)

Matrix- frames frequency of use				
Speeches	Eastern European migrants 2.8% (N = 73)		Middle Eastern migrants 97.2% (N = 1925)	
	Multicultural	Nationalistic	Multicultural	Nationalistic
Speech WW1	100% (N = 41)	0%	39.5% (N = 118)	60.5% (N = 181)
Speech WW2	–	–	–	–
Speech WW3	100% (N = 32)	0%	0%	100% (N = 403)
Speech MB1	–	–	9.5% (N = 16)	90.5% (N = 152)
Speech MB2	–	–	0%	100% (N = 126)
Speech MB3	–	–	0%	100% (N = 572)
Speech BS1	–	–	0%	100% (N = 269)
Speech BS2	–	–	0%	100% (N = 86)
Total (N = 1998)	100% (N = 73)	0% (N = 0)	7% (N = 134)	93% (N = 1791)

Source: Own elaboration

total number of words coded for this group of migrants (73), all fit in the multicultural frame.
- Of the words coded in the document that were about Middle Eastern migrants, 7% fit the multicultural frame and 93% fit the nationalistic frame. In other words, of a total of 1925 words coded for Middle Eastern migrants, 134 fit in the multicultural frame and 1791 fit in the nationalistic frame.

One reading of this would be that, in the period that included the 2015 migration crisis, Law and Justice politicians referred less to Eastern European migrants than Middle Eastern ones. The political speeches contain 2.8% of coding regarding Eastern European migrants and 93% regarding Middle Eastern migrants. It is perhaps not surprising that all the references to Eastern European migrants in these sources have multicultural rhetoric (100%) without any mention of security (0%). While some speeches may have an interesting percentage of the multicultural narrative in the case of Middle Eastern migrants, in most of them nationalistic rhetoric prevails (93%). In one speech (WW2), there is no mention of any group of migrants.

When it comes to the international prestige frame, the 'role of the state' category is the only narrative used for both groups of migrants (100% in both groups). When referring to providing refugee protection to both groups, Law and Justice politicians, at a very low rate, seek to show how Poland fulfils its obligations towards human rights protection and humanitarian law (see Fig. 8.1). It is important to add that even the appearance of this category is interesting in the case of Middle Eastern migrants, as the percentage for the multicultural frame is very low (7%), so one may conclude that it is not significant or representative of the whole notion of refugee protection for Middle Eastern migrants. Nevertheless, for both groups of migrants, respecting human rights and international law is for Law and Justice the main incentive to providing refugee protection.

a. *Politicians' speeches (PS)*[3]

According to Fig. 8.2, it is possible to speculate that Eastern European migrants are not viewed by the selected politicians as a security problem (0%). On the contrary, Middle Eastern migrants are considered a major

[3] See Index.

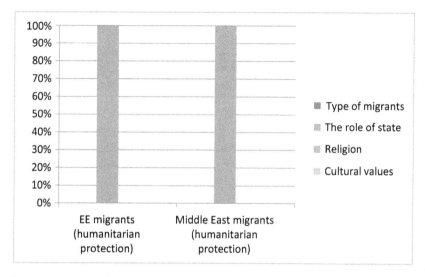

Fig. 8.1 Matrix frequency of international prestige benefit (PS). (Source: Own elaboration)

security issue. The 'role of the state' category represents Poland's political attitudes towards those migrants: anti-EU rhetoric, sovereignty discourse, nationalism, and so on (44.3%). This is the opposite of seeking international prestige, one may argue, as the benefits of security (defence) are very high (45.5%) and linked with the political actions (role of state), and both categories have the highest frequencies.

In the case of economic contribution (development benefit), as we may see in Fig. 8.3, there is just one mention of each group of migrants. In the case of Eastern European migrants, the 'role of the state' is the predominant category, while, on the other hand, it is even surprising to see a mention by the Minister of Interior, Mariusz Blaszczak (MB), of possible economic contributions.

In analysing the whole dataset, one may conclude that in migration parliamentary debates, the highest-level representatives of the Law and Justice party made very few (low) references to Eastern European migrants and but many (high) references to Middle Eastern migrants, especially from the security perspective. The humanitarian narrative in both groups is very low; nevertheless, when given it is within the context of an incentive of respecting international humanitarian norms.

8 EMPIRICAL RESULTS: THE (NON-) PROVISION OF REFUGEE PROTECTION 109

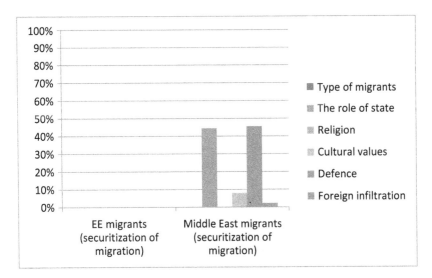

Fig. 8.2 Matrix frequency of the security benefit (PS). (Source: Own elaboration)

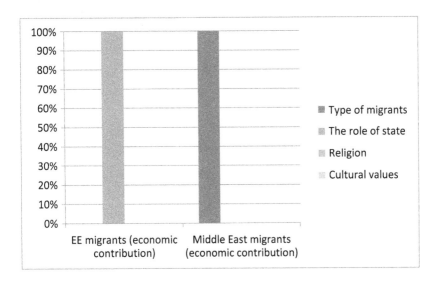

Fig. 8.3 Matrix frequency of the development benefit (PS). (Source: Own elaboration)

b. *Party manifestoes (PM)*[4]

The 2014 electoral campaign party manifesto made no reference to either group of migrants, so it was excluded as a source. This is presumably due to the scarce relevance of migration issues at the time to the PiS political interests. In 2015, with the migration-management crisis, the increase in the number of Ukrainians filing asylum applications and labour migrants coming to Poland, Law and Justice started to consider migration a political tool to express its concepts of the Polish nation (Table 8.3). The 2019 electoral party manifesto considers migration an important issue for PiS, but in which the use of a different narrative for Eastern European and Middle Eastern migrants is prevalent, as shown in Table 8.2:

In the 2019 party manifesto, all mention of Eastern European migrants is through a humanitarian narrative (100%), not an economic one (0%). It is interesting then to see how the group of Middle Eastern migrants is more coded (N = 395) than the Eastern European migrants (N = 114). As shown in Fig. 8.4, all mention, of the latter, match the incentive of fulfilling international law and human rights protection (the role of the state), so are defined as victims in search of protection. When it comes to Middle Eastern migrants, however, in the case of an altruistic public good, international recognition is the prevalent rhetoric. Nevertheless, it is worth pointing out that the reference to these migrants as victims in need of protection is minimal (N = 53) in comparison with the vision of them as a security problem (N = 342). In other words, the frequency in the multicultural frame would be 13.4% and, in the case of the nationalistic frame, 86.6%—again, a very low percentage for the multicultural frame.

Table 8.3 Matrix- frames frequency of use Party manifesto (PM)

Party manifesto	Eastern European migrants 22.4% (N = 114)		Middle Eastern migrants 77.6% (N = 395)	
	Multicultural	*Nationalistic*	*Multicultural*	*Nationalistic*
PM 2019	100%	0%	13.4%	86.6%
Total	100%	0%	13.4%	86.6%
(N = 509)	(N = 114)	(N = 0)	(N = 53)	(N = 342)

Source: Own elaboration

[4] See Appendix C.

8 EMPIRICAL RESULTS: THE (NON-) PROVISION OF REFUGEE PROTECTION   111

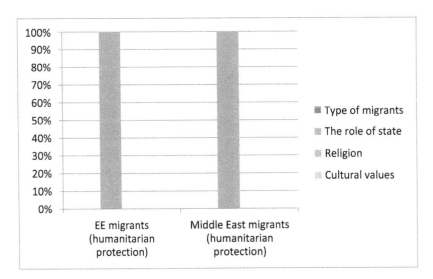

Fig. 8.4 Matrix frequency of the international prestige benefit (MP). (Source: Own elaboration)

As presented in Fig. 8.5, the PiS electoral party manifesto does not include any references to Eastern European migrants, while rhetoric about Middle Eastern migrants is highly securitised. This is supported by the much higher percentage of the nationalistic frame (86.6%) than the multicultural one (13.4%). In addition, the use of both the 'role of the state' ($N = 276$) and 'cultural values' ($N = 66$) frames show the relationship between the importance of cultural values in the party's political/policy documents (policy document and party manifesto), while, in the case of politicians' speeches, it is not mentioned at all.

In analysing the economic private good frame in Law and Justice's party manifesto, I did not find any reference to either group of migrants in economic terms. This provides convincing evidence of the securitisation migration narrative used by PiS as a political tool in its electoral campaign. Accordingly, no evidence of migration as an economic resource is reported in the electoral document.

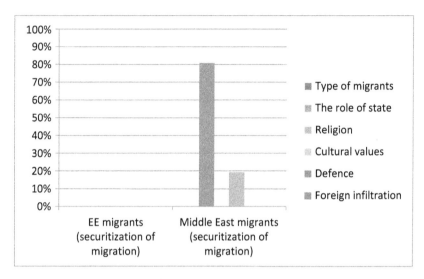

Fig. 8.5 Matrix frequency of the security benefit (PS). (Source: Own elaboration)

c. *Parliamentary debates*[5]

As mentioned previously, parliamentary debates with migration as the core of the discussion during 2015, 2016, and 2017 were selected. This period coincides with the events of the migration-management crisis and the adoption of the main migration and asylum legal measures by the EU.

Table 8.4 suggests that Eastern European migrants are barely mentioned in these parliamentary debates (8.3%); out of a total of 3060 words coded, just 278 words pertain to this group of migrants and all within the multicultural frame. Contrast this with references to Middle Eastern migrants, which are significantly present in the debates (93.6%), with a predominant security narrative (82.4%). In refugee protection terms, the highest frequency values, again in both groups, is the 'role of the state' category (see Fig. 8.6), which means that the incentive that motivates Poland to provide refugee protection or international protection is recognition, or prestige by respecting humanitarian and international law.

[5] See Appendix D.

8 EMPIRICAL RESULTS: THE (NON-) PROVISION OF REFUGEE PROTECTION   113

Table 8.4 Matrix- frames frequency of use Parliamentary debates (PD)

PDs	Eastern European migrants 6.2% (N = 253)		Middle Eastern migrants 93.6% (N = 2782)	
	Multicultural	Nationalistic	Multicultural	Nationalistic
PD 2015	100% (N = 61)	0%	17.1% (N = 94)	82.9% (N = 771)
PD 2016	100% (N = 97)	0%	10.1% (N = 88)	89.1% (N = 784)
PD 2017	100% (N = 95)	0%	24.6% (N = 198)	75.4% (N = 872)
Total (N = 3035)	100% (N = 253)	0% (N = 0)	16.9% (N = 380)	82.4% (N = 2427)

Source: Own elaboration

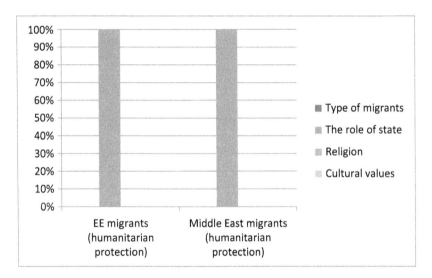

Fig. 8.6 Matrix frequency of the international prestige frame (PD). (Source: Own elaboration)

In parliamentary debates, the security narrative tends to focus on Poland's role in resolving the refugee crisis. In other words, in the case of Middle Eastern migrants, anti-EU rhetoric prevails, with an emphasis on Poland's sovereignty and national responses to the crisis. One may suggest that the role of the state (53.1%) in the security benefit frame refers to the benefit of the state in *not providing* refugee protection, that is, security and national responses. On the other hand, no mention of Eastern European migrants with a security narrative was reported (Fig. 8.7).

The results in Fig. 8.8 closely match those obtained by other data analysis using the economic private-good frame: Eastern European migrants are perceived as economic contributors, while Middle Eastern migrants are widely perceived as a security threat. In parliamentary debates, the predominant categories are the perception of the migrants as labour force (100%) and the role of Poland in acquiring this economic source (100%).

d. *Interviews*[6]

Interviews were conducted with Polish academics, politicians, and experts, all working with migration and asylum policy in Poland. The profile of the experts was classified into three categories:

1. Experts with knowledge of Eastern European migration in Poland;
2. Experts with experience/knowledge of Poland's position during the 2015 migration-management (refugee) crisis;
3. Experts with knowledge of national migration policy in relation to security;
4. Experts on Polish politics and populism.

The interviews were conducted via Skype (considered face-to-face). In order to maintain anonymity, each interviewee is coded as Expert (EX) with a number. It is important to point out for the final conclusions of the research that no Law and Justice politician I contacted and invited to an interview were willing to respond to questions. The interviews were used both to assess reflections of Law and Justice's concept of the Polish nation and as a data resource for content analysis. It is important to add that the coding process in interviews was not based on the respondents' own perceptions towards migration, but how they perceive Law and Justice's attitudes towards the different groups of migrants. The set of questions,[7] was operationalised with three parameters:

---

[6] See Appendix E.
[7] See Appendix F.

8 EMPIRICAL RESULTS: THE (NON-) PROVISION OF REFUGEE PROTECTION 115

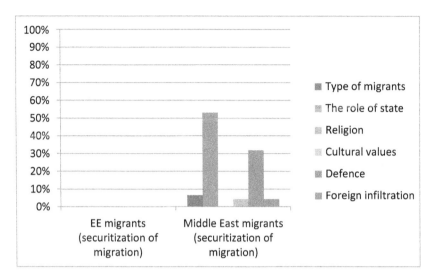

Fig. 8.7 Matrix frequency of the security benefit frame (PD). (Source: Own elaboration)

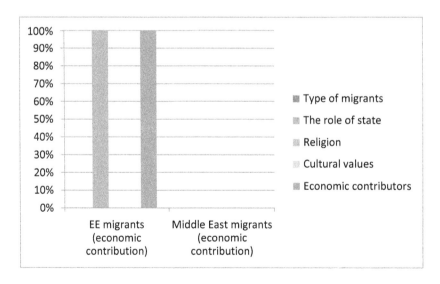

Fig. 8.8 Matrix frequency of the development benefit frame (PD). (Source: Own elaboration)

1. The EU-Poland relationship in the context of the 2015 crisis: In order to obtain information about how Law and Justice perceived the EU as the 'other' in identity terms, I used questions about how the party interacted with the EU in the case of refugee relocation;
2. National identity and perceptions towards migration: questions about to what extent Law and Justice seeks to re-conceptualise the idea of the Polish nation and how it may influence migration policy;
3. Security-humanitarian line—questions about Law and Justice's different perceptions towards Eastern European and Middle Eastern migrants from a humanitarian-security perspective.

The results in Table 8.5 generally agree with those obtained in previous data analysis: Eastern European migrants are mostly coded with a multicultural frame (**96.4%**), while Middle Eastern migrants are framed with a nationalistic narrative (**92.7%**).

Table 8.5 Matrix- frames frequency of use (I)

Interviewees	Eastern European migrants 70.8% (N = 3467)		Middle Eastern migrants 29.2% (N = 2283)	
	Multicultural	Nationalistic	Multicultural	Nationalistic
EX1	100% (N = 434)	0%	0%	100% (N = 1007)
EX2	100% (N = 336)	0%	0%	100% (N = 357)
EX3	100% (N = 230)	0%	36.4% (N = 99)	63.6% (N = 173)
EX4	100% (N = 457)	0%	–	–
EX5	100% (N = 428)	0%	0%	100% (N = 272)
EX6	100% (N = 436)	0%	–	–
EX7	71.5% (N = 549)	28.5% (N = 219)	0%	100% (N = 116)
EX8	100% (N = 406)	0%	0%	100% (N = 358)
Total (N = 5750)	96.4% (N = 3248)	3.6% (N = 219)	7.3% (N = 99)	93.9% (N = 2378)

Source: Own elaboration

8 EMPIRICAL RESULTS: THE (NON-) PROVISION OF REFUGEE PROTECTION

In regard to the 'international prestige' frame, again, we see the 'role of the state' category as the predominant one in both groups of migrants. In both cases, one could in fact state that fulfilling international law and respecting human rights is the main reason for why Law and Justice might provide international protection to refugees. In the case of Eastern European migrants, cultural values also play an important role for the party, accordingly related to its self-identification with the traditions and culture of these migrants. In the case of Middle Eastern migrants, however, security-related categories are much higher than the role of the state pertaining to the multicultural frame (Fig. 8.9).

When it comes to the security public good, in the case of Eastern European migrants, the most important categories are 'defence' and 'type of migrant'; however, the percentage of these migrants as a threat is very low (3.6%) and are mentioned with a nationalistic frame just by EX7. On the other hand, Middle Eastern migrants are highly perceived as a security threat (93.7%), with the 'role of the state' (37%) and 'cultural values' (26.5%), the highest categories (Fig. 8.10).

When it comes to the development benefit frame, Middle Eastern migrants are not referenced. Nevertheless, Eastern European migrants are

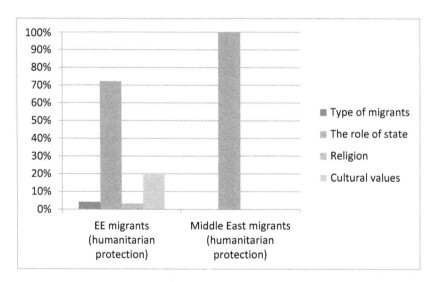

Fig. 8.9 Matrix frequency of the international prestige benefit frame (I). (Source: Own elaboration)

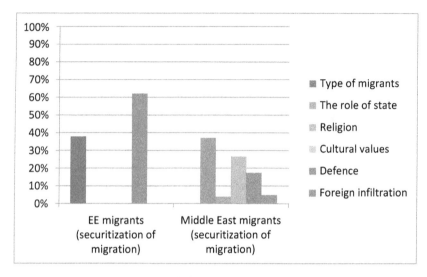

Fig. 8.10 Matrix frequency of the security benefit frame (I). (Source: Own elaboration)

perceived as a potential economic resource. This contrast becomes starker when one examines the high percentage of use of the 'type of migrant' category (70.2%). This category is related to perceptions of the typology of migrants, such as economic contributors (Fig. 8.11).

The content analysis of categories provides an overview about Law and Justice's different motivations towards the provision of public goods to migrants. This can be expressed in the following implicational statements:

- When it comes to Eastern European migrants, the predominant narrative is the multicultural one. For the Polish government, Eastern European migrants are perceived as, in the case of forced migration, victims to be protected and/or economic contributors.
- For Middle Eastern migrants, Law and Justice uses a nationalistic narrative rather than a multicultural one and they are considered either as a potential threat or economic resource for Poland.
- Law and Justice's main incentive is to gain international recognition by fulfilling international humanitarian law. This is provided by the predominance of the role of the state category (international recognition benefit frame).

8 EMPIRICAL RESULTS: THE (NON-) PROVISION OF REFUGEE PROTECTION   119

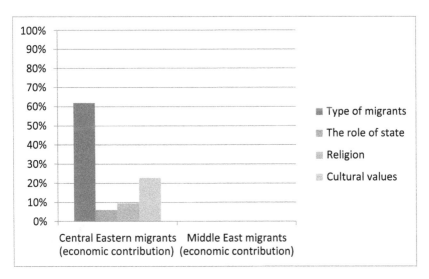

Fig. 8.11 Matrix frequency of the development benefit frame (I). (Source: Own elaboration)

- For the security benefit, I classify the results into two points: (A) in documents (party manifesto and policy document), the presence of the differences in cultural values with Middle Eastern migrants is important; (B) in political speeches and parliamentary debates, Law and Justice expresses more of an anti-EU rhetoric and the role of Poland towards those migrants, with an emphasis on internal security and defence. These findings may prompt plausible speculation that the 'role of the state' category from the 'securitisation of migration' sub-frame represents the benefit of not cooperating at the international level, or the benefit of providing internal security. In addition, categories such as 'defence' and 'cultural values', taken together, form different costs for Law and Justice, such as differences in culture, traditions, or perceptions of those migrants as a threat.
- In the dataset, except for the interviews, the predominant group referenced was from the Middle East. This may lead to the conclusion that the interviewees were more focused on emphasising how Eastern European migrants may be perceived from an identity perspective as closer to Poles for Law and Justice.

EASTERN EUROPEAN MIGRANTS: A MULTICULTURAL NARRATIVE

The analysis above strongly suggests that refugee protection is perceived in different ways, which strengthens the argument of the provision, or not, of different goods. In the case of this research data, Eastern European migrants comprise 33% of the total mentions by group of migrants in the analysed data (3874 words coded out of 11,009 words). The provision of refugee protection depends on the perceptions of the costs and benefits of it. While it may well be true that is it difficult to connect empirically from a qualitative perspective both the theoretical and case study parts, Table 8.5 shows how results coincide with the hypotheses of the cost-benefit calculus from the final public good provision. The percentage of the humanitarian protection frame is 98.7%, which supposes that almost in every case, Eastern European migrants who seek international protection are perceived by the Polish government as people who must be granted refugee status. The category that refers to gaining international prestige (the role of the state) is the most used, so one may conclude that the private incentive that motivates PiS to provide refugee protection is international recognition. Last but not least, the percentage of the 'securitisation of migration' frame is very low (1.2%). From this, the point is surely rather that Eastern European migrants are not perceived as a security threat (Table 8.6).

On the strength of these results, it is reasonable to conclude that, in the case of Eastern European migrants in danger (seeking protection), the PiS-led Polish government perceives the provision of refugee protection, and consequently, the benefits of fulfilling humanitarian law as much higher than the cost of a 'hypothetical' security threat.

Regarding development benefits, in the case of Eastern European migrants as economic contributors, from the total data, 75% of the coding of Eastern European migrants in references to Law and Justice's perceptions of those migrants are as an economic resource for Poland.

Table 8.7 appears to confirm that the Polish government considers Eastern European migrants as a potential labour force (economic migrants). The results shown in Fig. 8.12 provide definitive evidence of the hypotheses regarding Law and Justice's perceptions of Eastern European migration. The investigation reveals that these migrants are seen as asylum seekers or migrants who need to be granted the status of refugee and economic contributor. These perceptions are not excludable,

8 EMPIRICAL RESULTS: THE (NON-) PROVISION OF REFUGEE PROTECTION   121

Table 8.6   Matrix-frames frequency of use (data)-public goods

GOODS	Eastern European migrants 33% (N = 3874)	
	Altruistic public good	Security public good
FRAMES	Multicultural	Nationalistic
SUB-FRAMES	Humanitarian protection	Securitisation of migration
Data		
PS	100% (N = 32)	0%
PM	100% (N = 114)	0%
PD	100% (N = 102)	0%
I	94.7% (N = 1448)	4.6% (N = 219)
Total	98.7% (N = 1696)	1.2% (N = 219)

Source: Own elaboration

Table 8.7   Matrix- frames frequency of use (data)–development

Eastern European migrants 33% (N = 3874)	
FRAMES	Multicultural
SUB-FRAMES	Economic contribution
Data	
PS	100% (N = 41)
PM	0%
PD	100% (N = 151)
I	100% (N = 1828)
Total	75% (N = 2020)

Source: Own elaboration

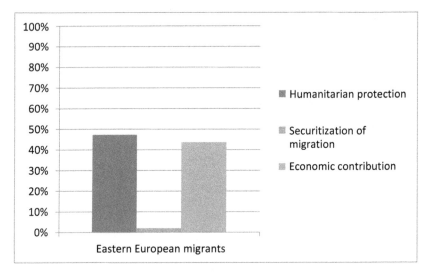

Fig. 8.12 Sub-frames for Eastern European migrants. (Source: Own elaboration)

rather it is not about these migrants' legal status but how PiS may perceive them, independent of their legal situation.

For Law and Justice, Eastern European migrants are close in identity terms to Poles. The idea of those migrants as victims and/or economic migrants led me to conclude that Law and Justice's perception of reality (norms and identities) shapes the production of this public good.

Middle Eastern Migrants: A Nationalistic Narrative

The results closely align, albeit inversely, with those obtained by the group of Eastern European migrants. As shown in Table 8.8, the 'humanitarian protection' frame has a very low rate (11.5%) in comparison to the 'securitisation of migration' frame, with a high percentage (88.5%).

These results have two meanings: (1) Law and Justice does not consider Middle Eastern migrants in general as forced migrants who need protection, with a very low percentage of them considered needing to be granted refugee protection (9.4%); (2) this group is rather seen as a threat

Table 8.8 Matrix-frames frequency of use (data)—public goods

GROUP OF MIGRANTS		
GOODS	Middle Eastern migrants 67% (N = 7135)	
	Altruistic public good	Security public good
FRAMES	Multicultural	Nationalistic
SUB-FRAMES	Humanitarian protection	Securitisation of migration
Data		
PS	4.8% (N = 118)	94.4% (N = 1809)
PM	13.4% (N = 53)	86.6% (N = 342)
PD	13.2% (N = 380)	86.8% (N = 2426)
I	6.1% (N = 99)	93.9% (N = 2378)
Total	9.4% (N = 650)	90.4% (N = 6955)

Source: Own elaboration

to the security of Poland. In public goods terms, the perceived benefits of providing refugee protection (international prestige) are less than the perceived costs of it (e.g., defence and differences in cultural values). During the 2015 refugee crisis, these sentiments led Poland to maintain an anti-refugee rhetoric, showing continuous opposition to the EU relocation efforts. Broadly speaking, in the whole analysis, there is a scant mention of these migrants as economic contributors, as shown in Table 8.9.

As predicted, these results coincide with the hypothesis that Middle Eastern migrants are not seen as an economic resource for Poland. As the table shows, of all the words coded about these migrants (7135), just 16 refer to them as economic migrants (4%).

Taken together in the sub-categories frame analysis, Fig. 8.13 can be used to emphasise that Middle Eastern migrants suppose a threat in Law and Justice's perceptions. One may conclude that for the party, these migrants do not fit its idea of the Polish nation and society as the 'cultural

Table 8.9 Matrix- frames frequency of use (data)–private good

Middle Eastern migrants 67% (N = 7135)	
FRAMES	*Multicultural*
SUB-FRAMES	*Economic contribution*
Data	
PS	100%
	(N = 16)
PM	0%
PD	0%
I	0%
Total	4%

Source: Own elaboration

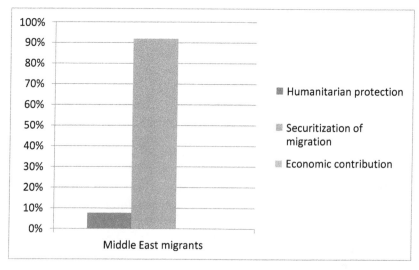

Fig. 8.13 Sub-frames for Middle Eastern migrants. (Source: Own elaboration)

values' are seen as completely different. In addition, there is no allowance for them to be economic contributors to Poland.

This graphic shows how the Polish government narrative with respect to these migrants is high securitised (91.9%). On the other hand, a very low percentage of the references are to migrants seeking international protection (8%). Last but not least, one may conclude that regarding labour migration, Law and Justice does not consider Middle Eastern migrants as desirable economic migrants (1%).

CHAPTER 9

Conclusion: Security and Humanitarian Preferences in Refugee Protection

This research offers a deep explanation of EU refugee governance dynamics through a public goods analysis. The case of Poland shows how the rational choice approach has shortcomings in explaining refugee protection burden-sharing. Refugee protection may be understood as an impure public good with partially public and private benefits. Political contestation is fundamental to understanding the provision of goods, in this case, norms, identities, and customs shape actors' preferences and utilities in the provision of public goods. A collective action dilemma, for instance, disagreement between the Member States on EU-wide refugee protection provision, is likely to happen when actors differ in their perceptions. For instance, sceptical political parties have a different vision of EU values than pro-integration political parties. In burden-sharing terms, cooperation between states is likely to happen when the sum of the benefits exceeds the costs to be shared by the states. This underlines the importance of the Member States' preferences in their decision-making to not cooperate in the refugee burden-sharing scheme during the 2015 mass-migration management crisis—some of them saw no reason to share the costs because they did not perceive any benefits at all. In this regard, refugee protection may emanate different benefits, and these benefits can be understood in terms of social construction. States may enhance their migration policies through perceived individual incentives; accordingly, the benefits analysed in this research, including international prestige and development, the

© The Author(s), under exclusive license to Springer Nature 127
Switzerland AG 2023
D. Caballero-Vélez, *Contesting Migration Crises in Central Eastern Europe*, Mobility & Politics,
https://doi.org/10.1007/978-3-031-44037-3_9

costs, and security threat perception provide knowledge about the Member States' rationales behind cooperating or not at the EU level on migration issues. While public goods have normally understood this through a rational-choice perspective, recent studies and this research show how understanding the constructivist nature of rational choice is crucial to analysing an actor's preferences and utility maximisation. In recent years, collective action literature is gaining importance due to its numerous implications in different areas of international relations and political science. In this literature, normally the question of why actors enhance some actions has been understood from a maximising- utility calculus model (rationalist approach). On the other hand, it helps also to understand why actors, in this case, states, prefer to take certain actions despite other seemingly contrary ones; consequently, this research applies an identity-utility model by which it is claimed that actors maximise their utility in carrying out actions influenced by their identities, which are constructed by their social realities.

EU refugee governance is marked by a security-humanitarian dichotomy in which Member States' national sovereignty and fulfilling European and international humanitarian law form what seems to be a never-ending dilemma for the functioning of the EU asylum system. As the EU attempts to find a solution, it has settled on a 'flexible solidarity' approach towards forced-displacement situations. Understanding the Member States' humanitarian-security dynamics may be analysed through a cost-benefit calculus model. In the case of Poland, we may conclude from the analysis of the perception of the costs and benefits that Law and Justice's vision of Poland strongly influences its political actions. The Polish government has different perceptions of different groups of migrants, and this depends on its partisan identity. Having specified this, migration as an issue of Law and Justice's identity is important here because, in this research, it is seen how the ruling party seeks to avoid EU values it does not appreciate and instead reinforces its idea of 'Polishness', which is nearer to the identity of the Visegrad Group (V4) countries. In this vein, Law and Justice's identification with the 'other' concept is reflected in its perceptions of migration: on the one hand, the ruling party in the Polish government has a preference for migrants from Eastern European countries, which it sees as closer to its idea of the Polish nation; on the other hand, the party is reluctant to relocate Middle East refugees in Poland as the EU, to some extent, is seen as imposing a 'Western vision' of what is correct to do, while the party perceives these migrants as conflicting with its vision of Poland. The CEE

Member States are motivated by the different perspectives of their realities—standing with the EU when migration is perceived as a 'hybrid war', for instance in the case of the Poland-Belarus border crisis, and by providing international protection to certain migrants, as in the case of Ukrainian refugees.

Developments viewed in isolation from earlier studies (migration studies, EU studies, political economy, etc.) are here considered together: the first of these is recent literature treating some areas of migration governance such as refugee protection and labour migration under public goods terms; second is a novel constructivist approach that seeks to provide insight into actors' identities in the construction of public goods; and, third, recent attempts by academics in understanding the EU's underintegration process in some policy domains. The multidisciplinary nature of the present thesis may have important implications for different areas of research: (1) migration studies; (2) public choice theory/public policy studies; or (3) EU studies/EU migration and asylum research. As with all such studies, this research has limitations that offer opportunities for further research. In this regard, based on the migration-public goods' literature, the identification of frame categories with the costs and benefits of the different public goods are in line with the theoretical assumptions of the altruistic/security public goods and the economy private good approaches. The question remains, however, whether such a category may be identified as a single cost-benefit calculation or different categories may be interpreted as comprising a perception that may represent a benefit or a cost. In the case of this project, I interpreted categories as 'perceptions' or 'feelings' identified with costs and benefits; for instance, in the role of the state regarding the altruistic public-good frame, it is obvious that one benefit that results from the state's motivations for protecting refugees is international recognition. Nevertheless, future research on identification with this benefit may be needed to contribute to the current model. When it comes to the case study (i.e., Law and Justice and migration as a specific policy domain), I have drawn a number of conclusions:

- Law and Justice enhances migration policy based on its partisan identity, and, accordingly, it has different visions depending on the type of migrant.
- Law and Justice's securitisation of migration is related to its perception of Arabic culture, traditions, and religion as incompatible with Polish 'traditional values'.

- Law and Justice has an 'open door' policy towards Eastern European migrants, perceived as labour migrants and/or refugees.

Another important point to mention is the interesting information provided by interviewees about Poland's response to the possible massive influx of migrants coming from Belarus to Poland. With the political tensions in Belarus, according to the information provided by respondents, the Polish government would likely be open to receiving Belarusians or to allocating them to Poland. This supports the findings that the Polish government has a 'dual approach towards migration'. In addition, as part of the analysis, it is important to point out the reluctance of Law and Justice politicians in being interviewed. From this, one may interpret to what extent Law and Justice representatives are against being asked about any question regarding migration as a sensitive topic related to security.

The questions raised by this study warrant further investigation into the possibility of applying this identity-utility model to other public goods' provision scenarios. Thus, the challenge for future research will be to apply this model to different case studies, in other words, different political parties or governments. By doing so, one might find political actors with different preferences in public policy choices, not only migration but also other policy domains. In addition, in line with the identity/utility analysis, it would be interesting to study to what extent populist political parties create concepts of nationhood by which public goods' provision is influenced. Although nation-state building literature has been widely used in migration studies, the concept of the 'nation-state-building process' has been interpreted quite often as a unique process in the construction of a state's formulation of its migration policy; accordingly, further research might be focused on understanding a state's national migration policies and studying nation- and state-building processes as two separate units of enquiry. On this subject, an identity-utility perspective would be of interest as a literature contribution in this field.

To sum up, the multidisciplinary nature of the present research (migration studies, European studies, political economy, etc.) may attract widespread interest among scholars from different fields. Despite the shortcomings of a lack of a deeper identification of the categories and the theoretical nature of the cost-benefit framework, this research provides a theoretical and methodological turning point in both public-goods and migration-studies literature. This main attempt of this research is to cover a number of aspects of governments' preferences towards the formulation of migration policies. In this regard, rather than engaging in the debate on populist political parties applying anti-migration rhetoric, I shed light on the rationales behind these political actors' preferences and actions with regard to migration.

Appendix A: Codebook

Categories' indicators

Sub-frames	Categories	Indicators
Economic contribution	Economic contributors	Labour migrants
		High –skilled migrants
	The role of state	Access to labour market Education
		Employment
	Same religion	Catholic values
		Same religious traditions Share Christian values
	Similar cultural values	Common Slavic identity Cultural similarities
		Equality
		Integration
		Similar historical roots Tolerance
Humanitarian protection	Type of migrants	Forced migrants Regular Vulnerable
	The role of state	Burden-sharing
		Cooperation EU and Member States
		Coordination
		Geneva Convention Globalization Human rights Humanitarian law
		International reputation
		Legality
		Relocation
		Rights' protection

(*continued*)

© The Author(s), under exclusive license to Springer Nature Switzerland AG 2023
D. Caballero-Vélez, *Contesting Migration Crises in Central Eastern Europe*, Mobility & Politics,
https://doi.org/10.1007/978-3-031-44037-3

(continued)

Categories' indicators

Sub-frames	Categories	Indicators
Securitisation of migration	Same religion	Catholic values Same religious traditions Share Christian values
	Similar cultural values	Common Slavic identity Cultural similarities Equality Integration Similar historical roots Tolerance
	Type of migrants	Africa Criminals Eastern-Central Illegal Middle East Terrorists
	The role of state	Anti-EU National response No burden-sharing No Poland's responsibility Our citizens Our nation Poland Sovereignty
	Religion	Catholicism Christian values Christianity Our religion
	Cultural values	No integration Our culture Our identity Polish culture Slavic identity Threat to our traditions
	Defence	Border control Internal security Political stability Return Threat to public order
	Foreign infiltration	Invasion Islam Muslim Organised crime Terrorism

Appendix B: Politicians' Speeches

(1) Forced Migration
(1.1) General frames of humanitarian and security narratives

Matrix- humanitarian and security narrative frames frequency of use

	GROUP OF MIGRANTS			
FRAMES	Eastern European migrants		Middle Eastern migrants	
	Multicultural	Nationalistic	Multicultural	Nationalistic
SUB-FRAMES	Humanitarian protection	Securitisation of migration	Humanitarian protection	Securitization of migration
Speeches				
Speech WW1	–	–	33.3% (N = 118)	60.5% (N = 181)
Speech WW2	–	–	–	–
Speech WW3	100% (N = 32)	0%	0%	100% (N = 403)
Speech MB1	–	–	0%	100% (N = 152)
Speech MB2	–	–	0%	100% (N = 126)
Speech MB3	–	–	0%	100% (N = 572)
Speech BS1	–	–	0%	100% (N = 289)
Speech BS2	–	–	0%	100% (N = 86)
Total	100% (N = 32)	0%	4.8% (N = 118)	94.4% (N = 1809)

© The Author(s), under exclusive license to Springer Nature Switzerland AG 2023
D. Caballero-Vélez, *Contesting Migration Crises in Central Eastern Europe*, Mobility & Politics,
https://doi.org/10.1007/978-3-031-44037-3

(1.2) Frame of the humanitarian narrative

Matrix- humanitarian narrative frame frequency

GROUP OF MIGRANTS

SUB-FRAMES	Eastern European migrants				Middle Eastern migrants			
	Humanitarian protection				Humanitarian protection			
Categories	Type of migrants	The role of state	Religion	Cultural values	Type of migrants	The role of state	Religion	Cultural values
Speeches								
Speech WW1	–	–	–	–	0%	100% (N = 188)	0%	0%
Speech WW2	–	–	–	–	–	–	–	–
Speech WW3	0%	100% (N = 32)	0%	0%	–	–	–	–
Speech MB1	–	–	–	–	–	–	–	–
Speech MB3	–	–	–	–	–	–	–	–
Speech MB4	–	–	–	–	–	–	–	–
Speech BS1	–	–	–	–	–	–	–	–
Speech BS2	–	–	–	–	–	–	–	–
Total	0%	100% (N = 32)	0%	0%	0%	100% (N = 118)	0%	0%

(1.3) Frame of the security narrative (Eastern European migrants)

Matrix- security narrative frame frequency (EE migrants)

GROUP OF MIGRANTS

    Eastern European migrants

SUB- FRAME	*Securitisation of migration*					
Categories	Type of Migrants	The role of state	Religion	Cultural values	Defence	Foreign infiltration
Speeches						
Speech WW1	–	–	–	–	–	–
Speech WW2	–	–	–	–	–	–
Speech WW3	–	–	–	–	–	–
Speech MB1	–	–	–	–	–	–
Speech MB2	–	–	–	–	–	–
Speech MB3	–	–	–	–	–	–
Speech DT1	–	–	–	–	–	–
Speech DS1	–	–	–	–	–	–
Speech DS2	–	–	–	–	–	–
Total	–	–	–	–	–	–

138　APPENDIX B: POLITICIANS' SPEECHES

(1.4) Frame of the security narrative (Middle Eastern migrants)

Matrix- security public good frame frequency (Middle Eastern migrants)

GROUP OF MIGRANTS

Middle Eastern migrants

SUB- FRAME Securitisation of migration

Categories	Type of migrants	The role of state	Religion	Cultural values	Defence	Foreign infiltration
Speeches						
Speech WW1	0%	0%	0%	0%	100% (N = 78)	0%
Speech WW2	–	–	–	–	–	–
Speech WW3	0%	68.6% (N = 232)	0%	0%	31.4% (N = 106)	0%
Speech MB1	0%	0%	0%	31.6% (N = 48)	68.4% (N = 104)	0%
Speech MB2	0%	0%	0%	23.8% (N = 30)	76.2% (N = 96)	0%
Speech MB3	0%	41.6% (N = 238)	0%	0%	42.8% (N = 245)	15.6% (N = 89)
Speech DS1	0%	100% (N=289)	0%	0%	0%	0%
Speech DS2	0%	100% (N = 86)	0%	0%	0%	0%
Total	0%	44.3% (N = 845)	0%	7.9% (N = 78)	45.5% (N = 629)	2.2% (N = 89)

APPENDIX B: POLITICIANS' SPEECHES 139

(2) Economic Migration
(2.1) General frames of the economic development narrative

Matrix- economic development narrative frames frequency of use

GROUP OF MIGRANTS		
FRAMES	Eastern European migrants	Middle Eastern migrants
	Multicultural	Multicultural
SUB-FRAMES	Economic contribution	Economic contribution
Speeches		
Speech WW1	100% (N = 41)	–
Speech WW2	–	–
Speech WW3	–	–
Speech MB1	–	100% (N = 16)
Speech MB2	–	–
Speech MB3	–	–
Speech DT1	–	–
Speech DS2	–	–
Total	100% (N = 41)	100% (N = 16)

(2.2) Frame of the economic development narrative (Eastern European migrants)

Matrix—economic development narrative frame frequency (EE migrants)

GROUP OF MIGRANTS				
	Eastern European migrants			
SUB- FRAME	Multicultural			
Categories	Economic contributors	The role of state	Religion	Cultural values
Speeches				
Speech WW1	0%	100% (N = 41)	0%	0%
Speech WW2	–	–	–	–
Speech WW3	–	–	–	–
Speech MB1	–	–	–	–
Speech MB2	–	–	–	–
Speech MB3	–	–	–	–
Speech DT1	–	–	–	–
Speech DS2	–	–	–	–
Total	0%	100% (N = 41)	0%	0%

140 APPENDIX B: POLITICIANS' SPEECHES

(2.3) Frame of the economic development narrative (Middle Eastern migrants)

Matrix- economic development narrative frame frequency

GROUP OF MIGRANTS

Middle Eastern migrants

SUB- FRAME	Multicultural			
Categories	Type of migrants	The role of state	Religion	Cultural values
Speeches				
Speech WW1	–	–	–	–
Speech WW2	–	–	–	–
Speech WW3	–	–	–	–
Speech MB1	100% (N = 16)	–	–	–
Speech MB3	–	–	–	–
Speech MB4	–	–	–	–
Speech DS1	–	–	–	–
Speech DS2	–	–	–	–
Total	100% (N = 16)	0%	0%	0%

Appendix C: Law and Justice Party Manifesto

(1) Forced Migration
(1.1) General frames of humanitarian and security narratives

Matrix- frames frequency of use

GROUP OF MIGRANTS				
FRAMES	Eastern European migrants		Middle East migrants	
	Multicultural	Nationalistic	Multicultural	Nationalistic
SUB-FRAMES	Humanitarian protection	Securitisation of migration	Humanitarian protection	Securitisation of migration
Party manifesto				
PM 2019	100% (N = 114)	0%	13.4% (N = 53)	86.6% (N = 342)
Total	100%(N = 114)	0%(N = 0)	13.4%(N = 53)	86.6%(N = 342)

© The Author(s), under exclusive license to Springer Nature
Switzerland AG 2023
D. Caballero-Vélez, *Contesting Migration Crises in Central Eastern Europe*, Mobility & Politics,
https://doi.org/10.1007/978-3-031-44037-3

(1.2) Frame of the humanitarian narrative

Matrix- humanitarian narrative frequency of use

GROUP OF MIGRANTS

SUB-FRAMES	Eastern European migrants				Middle East migrants			
	Humanitarian protection (N = 114)				Humanitarian protection (N = 53)			
Categories	Type of migrants	The role of state	Religion	Cultural values	Type of migrants	The role of state	Religion	Cultural values
Party manifesto PD 2019	0%	100% (N = 114)	0%	0%	0%	100% (N = 53)	0%	0%
Total	0% (N = 0)	100% (N = 114)	0% (N = 0)	0% (N = 0)	0% (N = 0)	100% (N = 53)	0% (N = 0)	0% (N = 0)

(1.3) Frame of the security narrative (EE migrants)

Matrix- security narrative frequency of use (EE migrants)

GROUP OF MIGRANTS

	Eastern European migrants						
SUB- FRAME	Securitisation of migration						
Categories	Type of migrants	The role of state	Religion	Cultural values	Defence	Foreign infiltration
Party manifesto PD 2019	–	–	–	–	–	–
Total	–	–	–	–	–	–

(1.4) Frame of the security narrative (Middle Eastern migrants)

Matrix: security narrative frequency of use (Middle Eastern migrants)

GROUP OF MIGRANTS

Middle East migrants

SUB-FRAME: Securitisation of migration (N = 342)

Categories	Type of migrants	The role of state	Religion	Cultural values	Defence	Foreign infiltration
Party manifesto PM 2019	0%	80.7% (N = 276)	0%	19.3% (N = 66)	0%	0%
Total	0% (N = 0)	80.7% (N = 276)	0% (N = 0)	19.3% (N = 66)	0% (N = 0)	0% (N = 0)

(2) Economic Migration
(2.1) General frames of the economic development narrative

Matrix- economic development narrative frequency of use

GROUP OF MIGRANTS		
	Eastern European migrants	Middle Eastern migrants
GOODS	Economy private good	Economy private good
FRAMES	Multicultural	Multicultural
SUB-FRAMES	Economic contribution	Economic contribution
Party manifesto PM 2019 Total	– –	– –

# Appendix D: Parliamentary Debates

(1) Forced Migration
(1.1) General frames of humanitarian and security approaches

Matrix- frames frequency of use

GROUP OF MIGRANTS

FRAMES	Eastern European migrants		Middle Eastern migrants	
	Multicultural	Nationalistic	Multicultural	Nationalistic
SUB-FRAMES	Humanitarian protection	Securitisation of migration	Humanitarian protection	Securitisation of migration
PDs				
PD 2015	100% (N = 61)	0%	10.9% (N = 94)	89.1% (N = 771)
PD 2016	–	–	10.1% (N = 88)	89.9% (N = 784)
PD 2017	100% (N = 41)	0%	18.5% (N = 198)	81.5% (N = 872)
Total	100% (N = 102)	0% (N = 0)	13.2% (N = 380)	86.8% (N = 2426)

© The Author(s), under exclusive license to Springer Nature
Switzerland AG 2023
D. Caballero-Vélez, *Contesting Migration Crises in Central Eastern Europe*, Mobility & Politics,
https://doi.org/10.1007/978-3-031-44037-3

(1.2) Frame of the humanitarian narrative

Matrix- humanitarian narrative frequency of use

GROUP OF MIGRANTS

SUB-FRAMES	Eastern European migrants				Middle Eastern migrants			
	Humanitarian protection (N = 102)				Humanitarian protection			
Categories	Type of migrants	The role of state	Religion	Cultural values	Type of migrants	The role of state	Religion	Cultural values
PDs								
PD 2015	0%	100% (N = 61)	0%	0%	0%	100% (N = 94)	0%	0%
PD 2016	–	–	–	–	0%	100% (N = 88)	0%	0%
PD 2017	0%	100% (N = 41)	0%	0%	0%	100% (N = 198)	0%	0%
Total	0% (N = 0)	100% (N = 102)	0% (N = 0)	0% (N = 0)	0% (N = 0)	100% (N = 380)	0% (N = 0)	0% (N = 0)

(1.3) Frame of the security narrative (Eastern European migrants)

Matrix- security narrative frequency of use (EE migrants)						
GROUP OF MIGRANTS						
	Eastern European migrants					
SUB- FRAME	Securitisation of migration					
Categories	Type of migrants	The role of state	Religion	Cultural values	Defence	Foreign infiltration
PDs						
PD 2015	–	–	–	–	–	–
PD 2016	–	–	–	–	–	–
PD 2017	–	–	–	–	–	–
Total	–	–	–	–	–	–

(1.4) Frame of the security narrative (Middle Eastern migrants)

Matrix- security narrative frequency of use (Middle Eastern migrants)						
GROUP OF MIGRANTS						
	Middle Eastern migrants					
SUB-FRAME	Securitisation of migration (N = 2426)					
Categories	Type of migrants	The role of state	Religion	Cultural values	Defence	Foreign infiltration
PDs						
PD 2015	14.6% (N = 110)	49.3% (N = 368)	0%	12.9% (N = 96)	17.6% (N = 131)	5.5% (N = 41)
PD 2016	4.2% (N = 34)	67.7% (N = 554)	0%	0%	28.1% (N = 230)	0%
PD 2017	0.7% (N = 8)	42.4% (N = 466)	0%	0%	49.6% (N = 545)	7.2% (N = 79)
Total	6.5% (N = 152)	53.1% (N = 1388)	0%	4.3% (N = 96)	31.8% (N = 906)	4.2% (N = 120)

(2) Economic Migration
(2.1) General frames of the economic development narrative

Matrix- general narrative frequency of use

GROUP OF MIGRANTS

	Eastern European migrants	Middle Eastern migrants
GOODS	Economy private good	Economy private good
FRAMES	Multicultural	Multicultural
SUB-FRAMES	Economic contribution	Economic contribution
PDs		
PD 2015	–	–
PD 2016	100% (N = 97)	0%
PD 2017	100% (N = 54)	0%
Total	100%(N = 151)	0%

(2.2) Frame of the economic development narrative (Eastern European migrants)

Matrix- economic development frame frequency (EE migrants)

GROUP OF MIGRANTS

	Eastern European migrants			
SUB- FRAME	Economic contribution (N = 151)			
Categories	Economic contributors	The role of state	Religion	Cultural values
PDs				
PD 2015	–	–	–	–
PD 2016	0%	100% (N = 97)	0%	0%
PD 2017	100% (N = 54)	0%	0%	0%
Total	100% (N = 54)	100% (N = 97)	0% (N = 0)	0% (N = 0)

Appendix E: Interviews

(1) Forced Migration
(1.1) General frames of humanitarian and security narratives

Matrix-humanitarian and security narratives frames frequency of use

GROUP OF MIGRANTS				
FRAMES	Eastern European migrants		Middle Eastern migrants	
	Multicultural	Nationalistic	Multicultural	Nationalistic
SUB-FRAMES	Humanitarian protection	Securitisation of migration	Humanitarian protection	Securitisation of migration
Interviewees				
EX1	100% (N = 231)	0%	0%	100% (N = 1007)
EX2	100% (N = 171)	0%	0%	100% (N = 357)
EX3	100% (N = 26)	0%	36.4% (N = 99)	63.6% (N = 173)
EX4	–	–	–	–
EX5	100% (N = 114)	0%	0%	100% (N = 272)
EX6	100% (N = 241)	0%	–	–
EX7	63.2% (N = 376)	36.8% (N = 219)	0%	100% (N = 116)
EX8	100% (N = 289)	0%	0%	100% (N = 358)
Total	94.7% (N = 1448)	4.6% (N = 219)	6.1% (N = 99)	93.9% (N = 2378)

© The Author(s), under exclusive license to Springer Nature Switzerland AG 2023
D. Caballero-Vélez, *Contesting Migration Crises in Central Eastern Europe*, Mobility & Politics,
https://doi.org/10.1007/978-3-031-44037-3

(1.2) Frame of the humanitarian narrative

Matrix- humanitarian narrative frame frequency

GROUP OF MIGRANTS

SUB-FRAMES	Eastern European migrants				Middle Eastern migrants			
	Humanitarian protection				Humanitarian protection			
Categories	Type of migrants	The role of state	Religion	Cultural values	Type of migrants	The role of state	Religion	Cultural values
Interviewees								
EX1	0%	82.3% (N = 190)	17.8% (N = 41)	0%	–	–	–	–
EX2	28.7% (N = 49)	0%	0%	71.4% (N = 122)	–	–	–	–
EX3	0%	100% (N = 26)	0%	0%	0%	100% (N = 99)	0%	0%
EX4	–	–	–	–	–	–	–	–
EX5	0%	100% (N = 114)	0%	0%	–	–	–	–
EX6	0%	100% (N = 241)	0%	0%	–	–	–	–
EX7	0%	46.8% (N = 200)	0%	53.2% (N = 176)	–	–	–	–
EX8	0%	77.2% (N = 223)	4.8% (N = 14)	18% (N = 52)	–	–	–	–
Total	4.1% (N = 49)	72.3% (N = 994)	3.2% (N = 55)	20.4% (N = 350)	0%	100% (N = 99)	0%	0%

(1.3) Frame of the security narrative (Eastern European migrants)

Matrix- security narrative frame frequency

GROUP OF MIGRANTS

Eastern European migrants

SUB- FRAME	Securitisation of migration					
Categories	Type of migrants	The role of state	Religion	Cultural values	Defence	Foreign infiltration
Interviewees						
EX1	–	–	–	–	–	–
EX2	–	–	–	–	–	–
EX3	–	–	–	–	–	–
EX4	–	–	–	–	–	–
EX5	–	–	–	–	–	–
EX6	–	–	–	–	–	–
EX7	37.9% (N = 83)	0%	0%	0%	62.1% (N = 136)	0%
EX8	–	–	–	–	–	–
Total (N = 219)	37.9% (N = 83)	–	–	–	62.1% (N = 136)	–

(1.4) Frame of the security public good (Middle Eastern migrants)

Matrix: security public narrative frame frequency

GROUP OF MIGRANTS

Middle Eastern migrants

SUB-FRAME *Securitisation of migration*

Categories	Type of migrants	The role of state	Religion	Cultural values	Defence	Foreign infiltration
Interviewees						
EX1	8.9% (N = 90)	65.8% (N = 665)	17.9% (N = 181)	0% (N = 177)	7.4% (N = 75)	0%
EX2	0%	11.8% (N = 42)	3.6% (N = 13)	40.6% (N = 145)	44% (N = 157)	0%
EX3	23.1% (N = 40)	76.9% (N = 133)	0%	0%	0%	0%
EX4	–	–	–	–	–	–
EX5	30% (N = 81)	11% (N = 30)	2.6% (N = 7)	40.1% (N = 109)	16.5% (N = 45)	0%
EX6	–	–	–	–	–	–
EX7	0%	0%	0%	78.5% (N = 91)	21.6% (N = 25)	0%
EX8	0%	56.4% (N = 202)	0%	0%	14.5% (N = 52)	29.1% (N = 104)
Total	10.3% (N = 211)	37% (N = 1072)	4% (N = 201)	26.5% (N = 522)	17.3% (N = 354)	4.9% (N = 104)

APPENDIX E: INTERVIEWS 153

(2) ECONOMIC MIGRATION
(2.1) General frames of the economic development narrative

Matrix- economic development narrative frames frequency of use

GROUP OF MIGRANTS

FRAMES	Eastern European migrants	Middle Eastern Migrants
	Multicultural	*Multicultural*
SUB-FRAMES	Economic contribution	Economic contribution
Interviewees		
EX1	100% (N = 203)	–
EX2	100% (N = 165)	–
EX3	100% (N = 204)	–
EX4	100% (N = 457)	–
EX5	100% (N = 314)	–
EX6	100% (N = 195)	–
EX7	100% (N = 173)	–
EX8	100% (N = 117)	–
Total (N = 1828)	100% (N = 1828)	–

(2.2) Frame of the economic development narrative (Eastern European migrants)

*Matrix- economic development narrative frame frequency
(EE migrants)*

GROUP OF MIGRANTS

Eastern European migrants

SUB-FRAME: *Multicultural*

Categories	Economic contributors	The role of state	Religion	Cultural values
Interviewees				
EX1	52.1% (N = 139)	0%	24% (N = 64)	24% (N = 64)
EX2	100% (N = 165)	0%	0%	0%
EX3	48.4% (N = 109)	30.7% (N = 69)	2.2% (N = 5)	18.7% (N = 42)
EX4	60.6% (N = 277)	16.2% (N = 74)	23.2% (N = 106)	0%
EX5	82.5% (N = 259)	0%	0%	17.5% (N = 55)
EX6	68.7% (N = 134)	0%	0%	31.3% (N = 61)
EX7	49.1% (N = 85)	0%	0%	50.8% (N = 88)
EX8	100% (N = 117)	0%	0%	0%
Total	70.2% (N = 1285)	5.9% (N = 143)	6.2% (N = 175)	17.8% (N = 310)

Appendix F: Interviews' Scenario

INTERVIEWS' SCENARIO

SECTION 1: INTRODUCTION/ GENERAL QUESTIONS ABOUT THE REFUGEE CRISIS

1.1. INTRODUCTION: RESPONDANT PROFILE

1. Please tell me about your work since 2011? What positions have you held since then in the party (*if our respondent is a member of the party*) and/or in a professional life? Did they relate to migration, asylum, borders, security, integration?
    a. *If our respondent is a member of the party, we can ask: When and how did you become a Member of PiS? What was your motivation to join the party and why did you chose PiS?*
2. What were/ are your responsibilities and tasks? Did they concern/ do they concern migration, asylum?

1.2. GENERAL QUESTIONS ABOUT THE REFUGEE CRISIS

If our respondent is expert, NGO practitioner, researcher, NOT POLITICIANS
1. What is your overview of the recent situation of migration and asylum in Europe? How has it changed since 2011? What do you know about the refugee crisis in Europe? Please elaborate on it in terms of:
    a. time range of the crisis
    b. geographic scope of the crisis
    c. key numbers / statistics about the crisis

2. What would be the difference between: an economic migrant, a refugee and an asylum-seeker?

3. Do you think that the increased number of migrants/refugees has already affected/ can affect the economy of your country? How, in what way?

If the answer is yes...
a) How can it be beneficial?
If the answer is not...
b) Why not?

4. Do you think the increased number of migrants/refugees can affect your country in terms of security/safety? What do you mean by security and safety? In what way it was affected? Could you please provide some examples?

If the answer is yes....
a) Do you think the level of crime may rise and if yes, why?
b) Do you think that there may be a real threat/risk of a terrorist attack?
c) Do you think migrants/ refugees may put in danger the identity/religion/culture of your country?

APPENDIX F: INTERVIEWS' SCENARIO   157

If the answer is no....
Do you think that migrants / refugees can be integrated in your country in terms of culture and socio-economic?

SECTION 2: NATIONAL MIGRATION/ ASYLUM POLICY AND BORDER CONTROL

1. Have the border controls become more restrictive due to the refugee crisis? In what sense? Could you please provide some examples?

2. Have there been taken any urgent national measures to regulate the increased number of migrants/refugees ? What kind of measures (e.g. legal, political)?
   [in Poland ask about legal changes]

SECTION3: REFUGEE PROTECTION AND POLITICAL ECONOMY

What do you understand by "refugee protection"? Do you know if there is any official definition/understanding of this expression in your country?
What is the legal framework for providing refugee protection in your country? To what extent it is rooted/based on:
- International
- EU
- National
Legislation?

REFUGEE PROTECTION

A) REFUGEE PROTECTION AS PUBLIC GOOD

In the case of both Middle East and Central Eastern European....

- **BENEFITS**

[Excludable altruistic benefits]
1. Do you think that that providing refugee protection, it fulfils moral and legal humanitarian obligations?

- **COSTS**

[State-specific security cost]
2. Do you think that providing refugee protection may lead to a security threats in your country?

B) REFUGEE PROTECTION AS NOT A GLOBAL PUBLIC GOOD

In the case of both Middle East and Central Eastern European

- **BENEFITS**

[State-specific security benefits]
3. Do you think that restrictive national asylum policy and border control may be beneficial for the security of your country?

- **COSTS**

[Prestige/humanitarian costs]
4. Do you think that it is better not to provide refugee protection and maintain a restrictive asylum policy even if its cost is to have less prestigious in the EU?

LABOUR MIGRATION

A) **LABOUR MIGRATION AS PRIVATE GOOD**

In the case of both Middle East and Central Eastern European

- **BENEFITS**

[Excludable benefits]
5. Do you think that when your country accepts migrants, it is related to increase the economy of the country?

- **COSTS**

[State-specific security cost]
6. Do you think that labour migrants may be seen as a threat to the society?

C) **GENERAL QUESTION**

B) In general terms, do you think that providing refugee protection is a cost or a benefit?

SECTION 4: NATIONAL IDENTITY AND PERCEPTIONS TOWARDS MIGRATION

1. Do you think that that idea of Poland influences in Polish migration politics? How?

1. Do you think that your political party narrative makes difference, and if yes, what, differences among asylum seekers/ refugees coming from the Middle-East and Central Eastern European?
[*In the case of Poland ask for Russians and Ukranians*]

2. In terms of identity, do you think that your political party creates a difference about migrants coming from Central Eastern European countries (closer to Polish society) rather than migrants coming from Middle East countries?

APPENDIX F: INTERVIEWS' SCENARIO   159

If the answer is yes...
   a. In which aspects? (religion, historical roots, traditions, etc.)

If the answer is no...
   b. Why not?

3. Do you think that migrants/refugees from Central-Eastern European countries have a greater capacity of integration in Poland?

4. Do you think migrants from Central Eastern European countries may contribute more to the Polish economy than migrants from Middle-East countries?

   If the answer is yes...
   a. Is it correlated of having a similar tradition/culture/identity?

5. Do you think migrants' religion is an important factor of integration in Poland?

   If the answer is yes...
   a. Catholic/Christian migrants are more likely to integrate rather than Muslim ones?

SECTION 5: BURDEN SHARING AND EU COOPERATION (EU-identity)

1. Do you see that your political party seed asylum seekers / refugees as a burden? Why?

   If the answer is yes...
   1. In order to cooperate at EU level, would be important to consider asylum/refugees as a burden?
   Do you see refugee protection burden-sharing as a duty?

2. What do you know about the 2015 Refugee Emergency Relocation Scheme?
   -What do you think about it? What was tour country stance on it?

3. Do you think that your country has enhanced efforts to cooperate for a more integrative Common European Asylum System? Why not/How?

4. Do you think an integrative/developed CEAS may be important to deal with migration/asylum issues in general, and, the massive influx of migrants in particular? Why?

5. Do you think that cooperation among Member States is important to deal with migration/asylum issues or, is it better to act with national responses?
   C) What would be a collective incentive to cooperate at EU level in asylum and migration issues?

INDEX

A
Aggregation technology, 16
Altercasting, 32, 35–41, 104
Amsterdam Treaty, 1, 45
Asylum and migration policy, 6
Asylum governance, 8
Asylum policy, 3, 68, 97, 114

B
Burden-sharing, 19, 22, 49, 69, 96, 100, 127

C
Civic Platform (*Platforma Obywatelska*, PO), 69, 76
Club goods, 14–15, 47
Collective action, 6, 11, 12, 14, 17, 19, 21, 28, 38, 47, 66, 127, 128
Collective action failures, 19, 22, 49
Collective action problem, 12, 18, 22
Collective action theory, 8
Collective good, 8, 37

Common European Asylum System (CEAS), 4
Common goods, 14
Common Security and Defence Policy (CSDP), 3–4
Congestion problem, 15
Constructivism, 28, 31, 91
Constructivist identity-utility model, 34
Cost-benefit, 7, 9, 29, 37, 49, 66, 71, 72, 91, 120, 128–130

D
Democratic Left Alliance (*Sojusz Lewicy Demokratycznej*, SLD), 75
Dublin Convention, 2, 3
Dublin Regulation, 2, 7

E
EU asylum law, 6
European asylum governance, 5
European asylum policy, 6

INDEX

European asylum regime, 7
European asylum system, 1, 69
European integration, 1, 3, 6, 7, 45, 93
Excludability, 14

F
Flexible solidarity, 4, 66, 72, 128
Forced migration, 8, 49, 70, 98, 118
Foreign policy, 3, 68
Freedom Union (*Unia Wolności*, UW), 76
Free ride, 22
Free-riding, 6, 17, 22
Free-riding problem, 13, 17, 19, 50

G
Global goods, 16
Globalness, 12, 15, 50
Global public goods, 21, 47, 49–51
Group size paradox, 36
Group-size premise, 39

H
Humanitarian protection, 7, 8, 94, 96, 99, 120, 122

I
Identity-utility, 32, 130
The identity-utility model, 33–36, 41, 92, 94–99, 101, 128, 130
Impure public good, 50, 127
International Organization for Migration (IOM), 48
International protection, 8, 67, 71, 92, 96, 98, 101, 103, 112, 117, 120, 125, 129
International public good, 8

J
Joint product model, 13, 50

L
Labour migration, 8, 98, 125, 129
Law and Justice (*Prawo i Sprawiedliwość*, PiS) party, 4, 68, 69, 76, 92, 97–99, 103–105, 107, 108, 110, 111, 114, 116–120, 122, 123, 125, 128–130
League of Polish Families (*Liga Polskich Rodzin*, LPR), 77
Logic of appropriateness, 32, 39

N
National public goods, 17
Negative selective incentives, 18
New institutionalism, 5–7, 33
New Pact on Migration (NPM), 4, 66
Non-excludability, 13
Non-excludable, 13
Non-excludable benefits, 18
Non-rivalrous, 13, 15

P
Pareto's efficiency premise, 36
Polishness, 75, 97, 128
Polish Peasant Party (*Polskie Stronnictwo Ludowe*, PSL), 75, 76
Polish People's Republic (PRL), 74
Polska Zjednoczona Partia Robotnicza (PZPR), 74, 75
Positive externalities, 12
Positive selective incentives, 18
Prisoners' dilemma, 19
Private goods, 13–14, 47, 111, 124, 129

Public goods, 6–8, 11, 12, 19–22, 28, 33, 36–39, 41, 47, 66, 92, 94, 98, 100, 101, 110, 117, 118, 120–123, 127–130
Public goods theory, 7, 27, 92, 98
Publicness, 12, 15, 22, 50
Pure public benefits, 19
Pure public goods, 13

R
Rational choice, 5, 7, 8, 27–31, 33, 92, 127, 128
Rational choice institutionalism, 5
Refugee deterrence, 9
Refugee protection, 7–9, 46, 49, 50, 65–72, 91–101, 103–125
Regional public goods, 16–17, 22
Responsibility-sharing, 8

S
Schengen Convention, 1, 45
Self-Defence (*Samoobrona Odrodzenie*, SO), 76
Social constructivism, 8, 9

Social dilemma, 19, 22
Solidarity, 4, 65, 66, 70, 71
Solidarity Electoral Action (*Akcja Wyborcza*, AWS), 75
Solidarność, 75
Spillover, 16, 17, 22
Subsidiarity, 15

T
Temporary protection, 1
Transnational public goods, 16, 17
2015 relocation scheme, 4
2016 Global Strategy for Foreign and Security Policy, 4

U
United Nations High Commissioner for Refugees (UNCHR), 48
Utility, 27, 29, 32, 34, 37, 66, 94, 127, 128, 130

V
V4 countries, 4, 128